Jumbo Coloring Pad
Animals

Coloring Pages for Kids

Coloring Pages for Kids
An imprint of Ciparum LLC

Jumbo Coloring Pad Animals
© 2017 Ciparum LLC
ISBN-10:1-63589-343-7
ISBN-13:978-1-63589-343-4

Coloring Pages for Kids

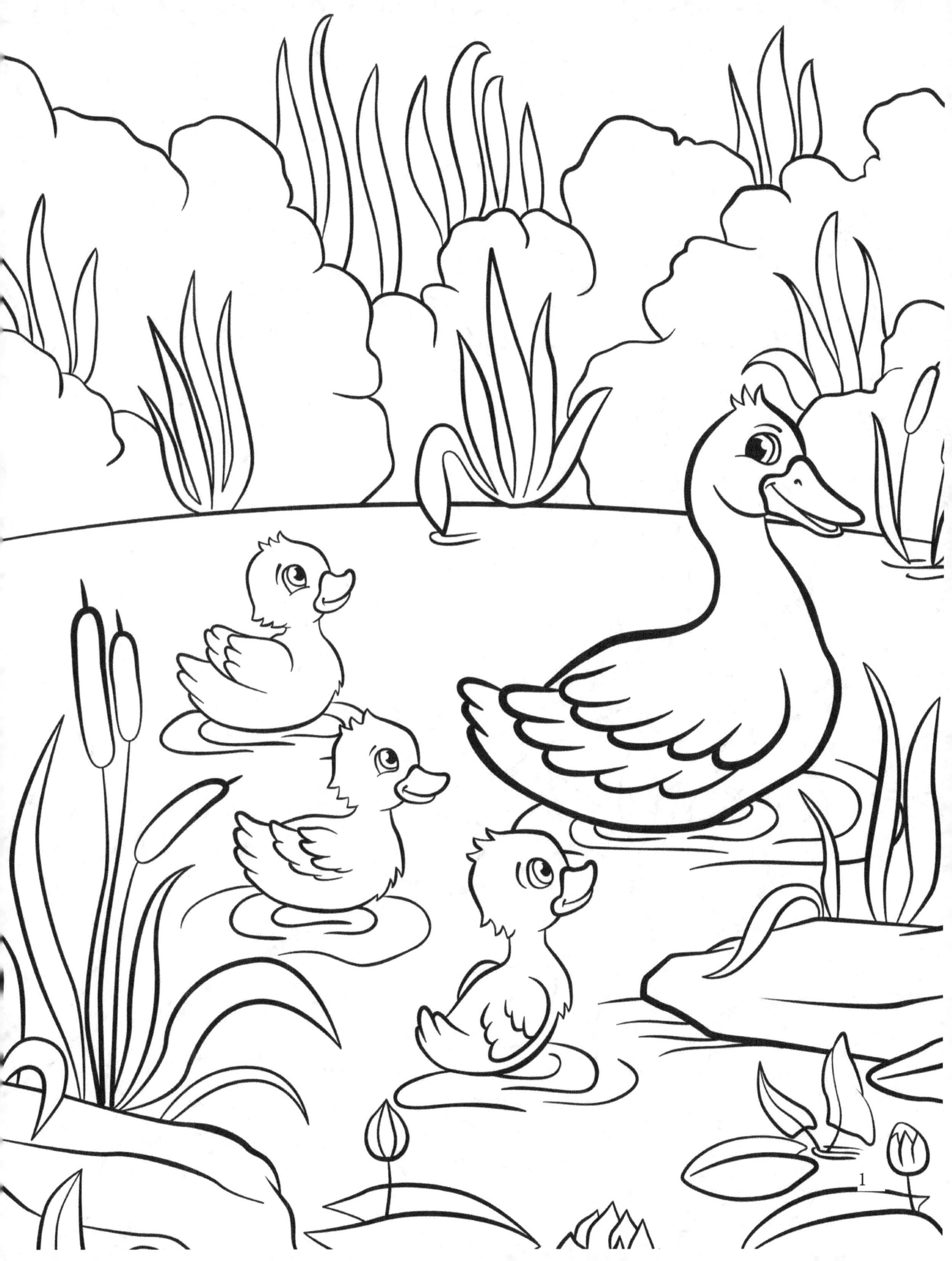

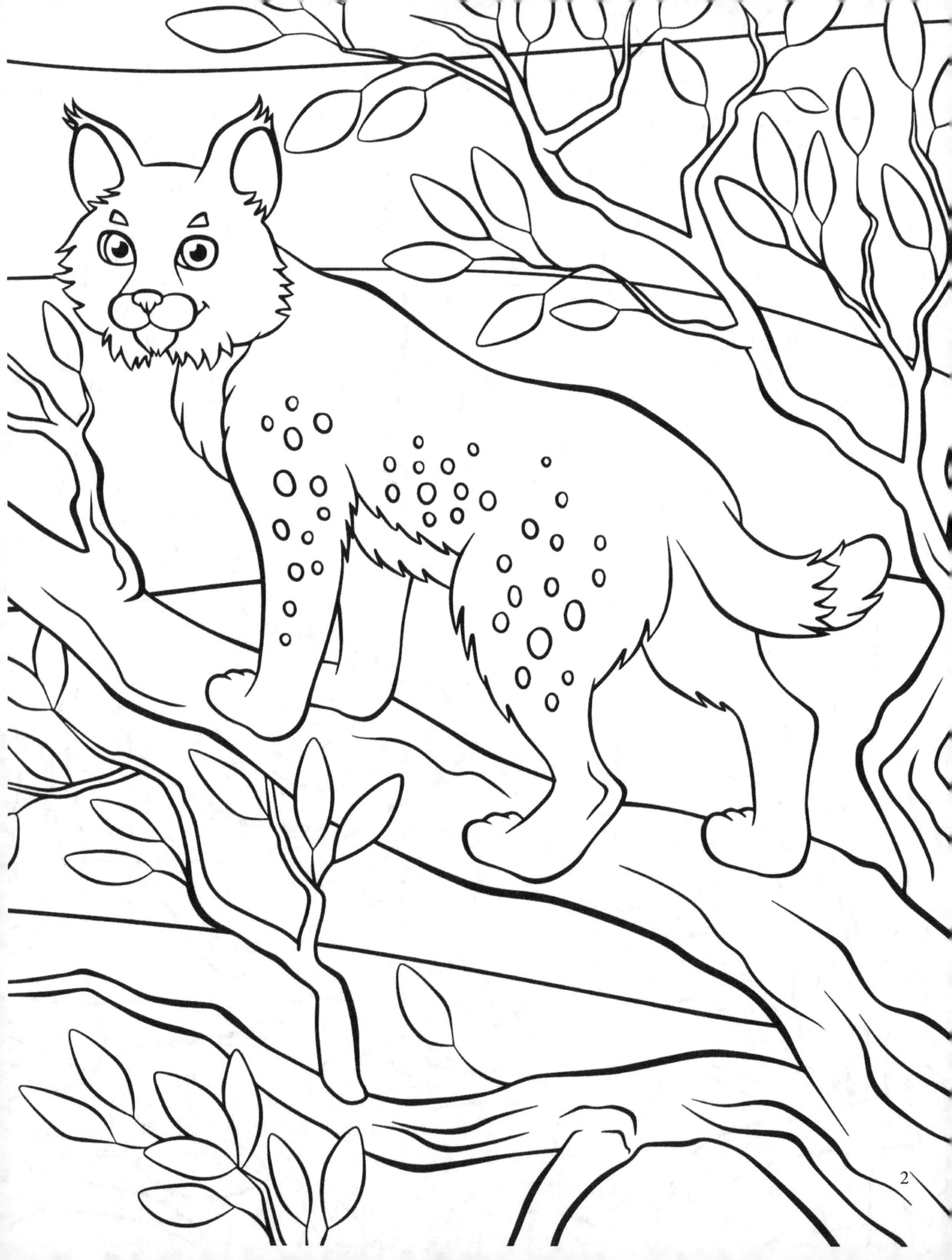

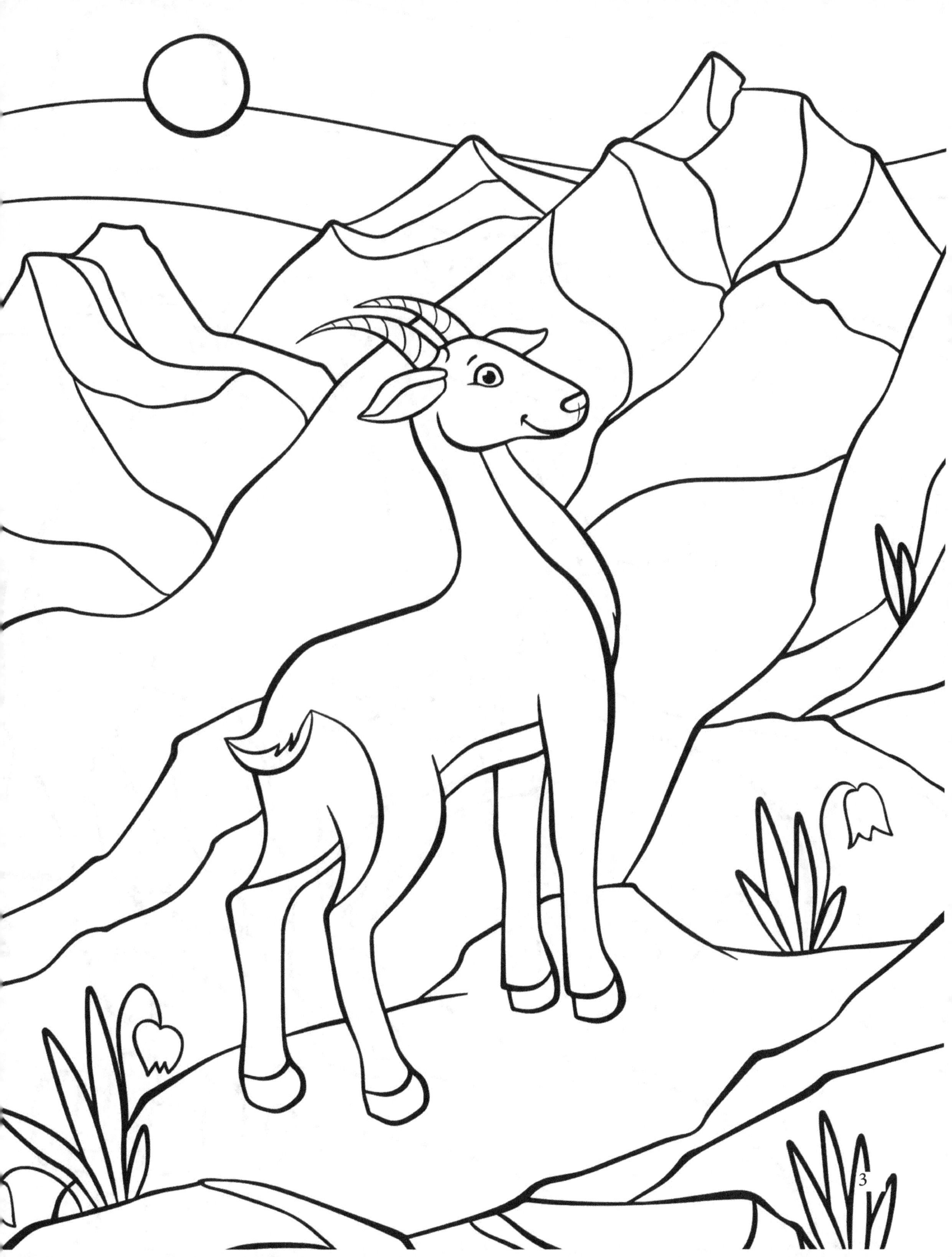

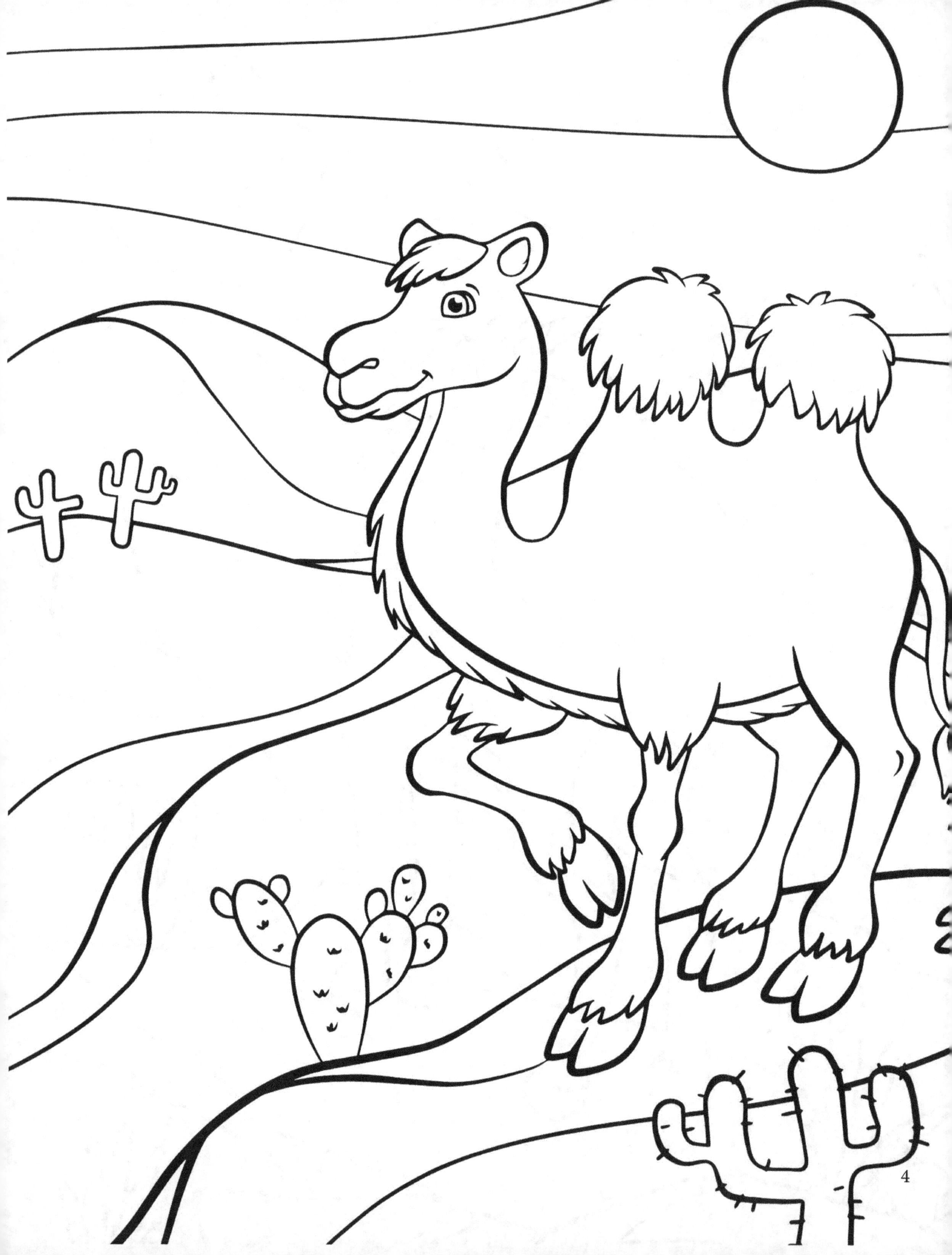

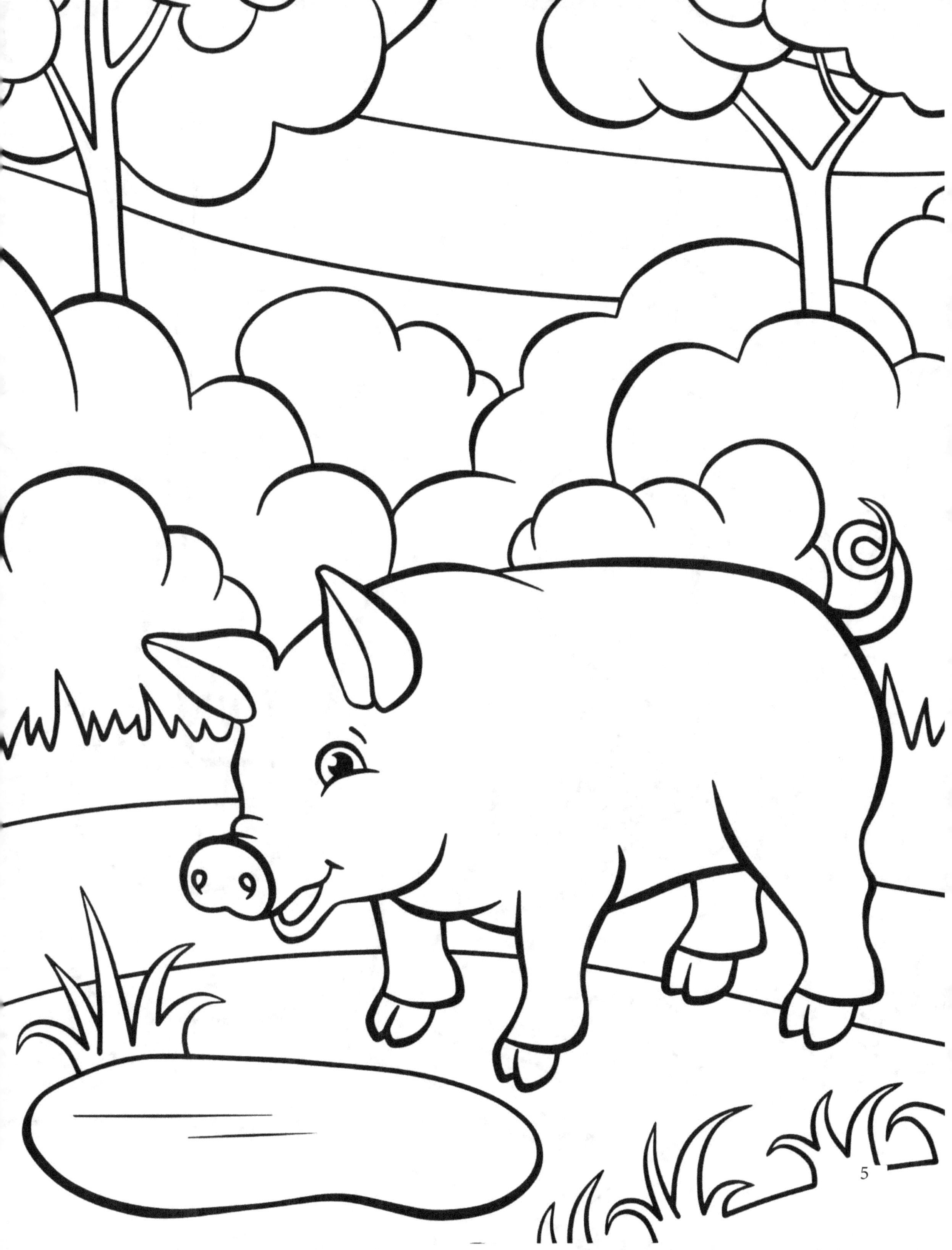

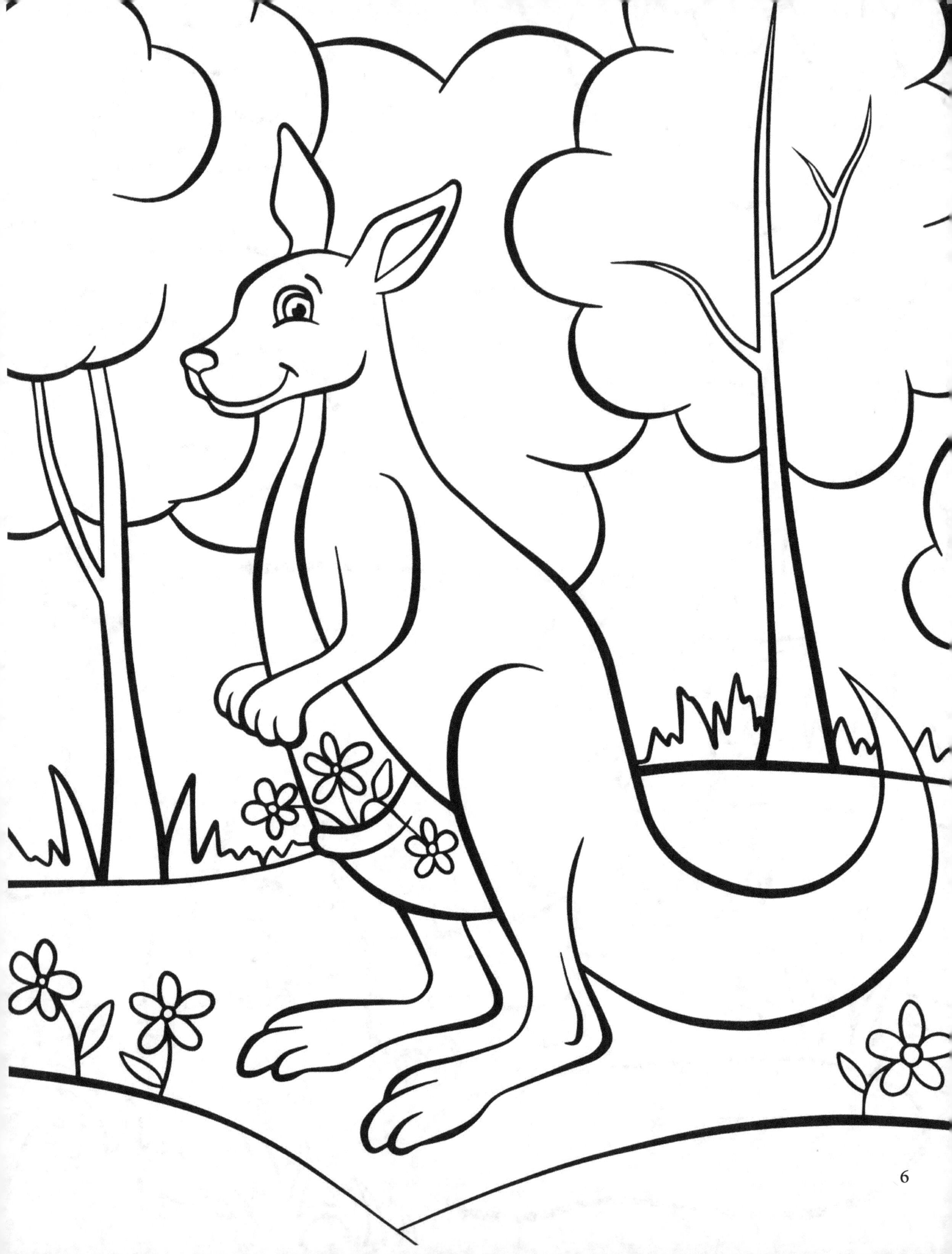

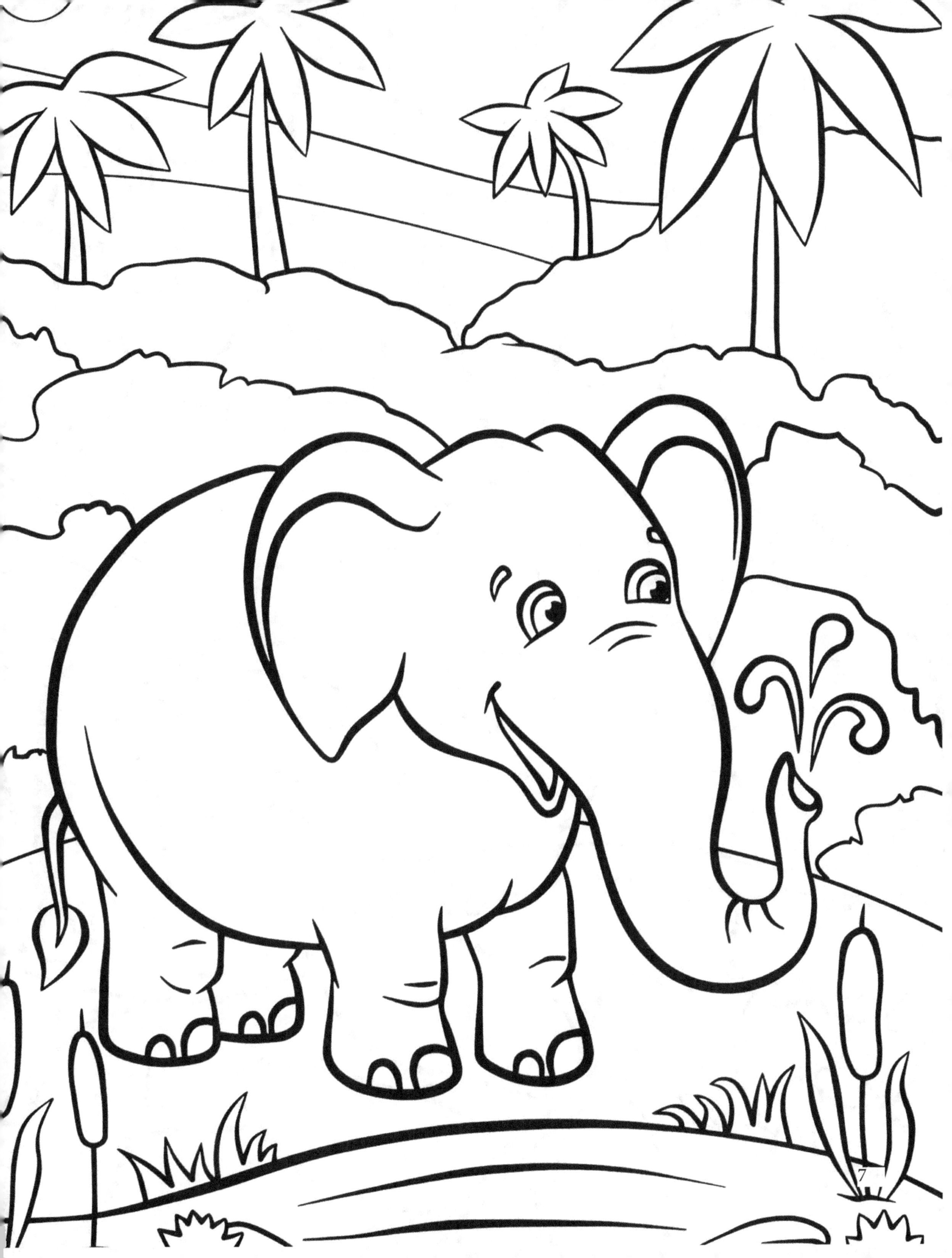
7

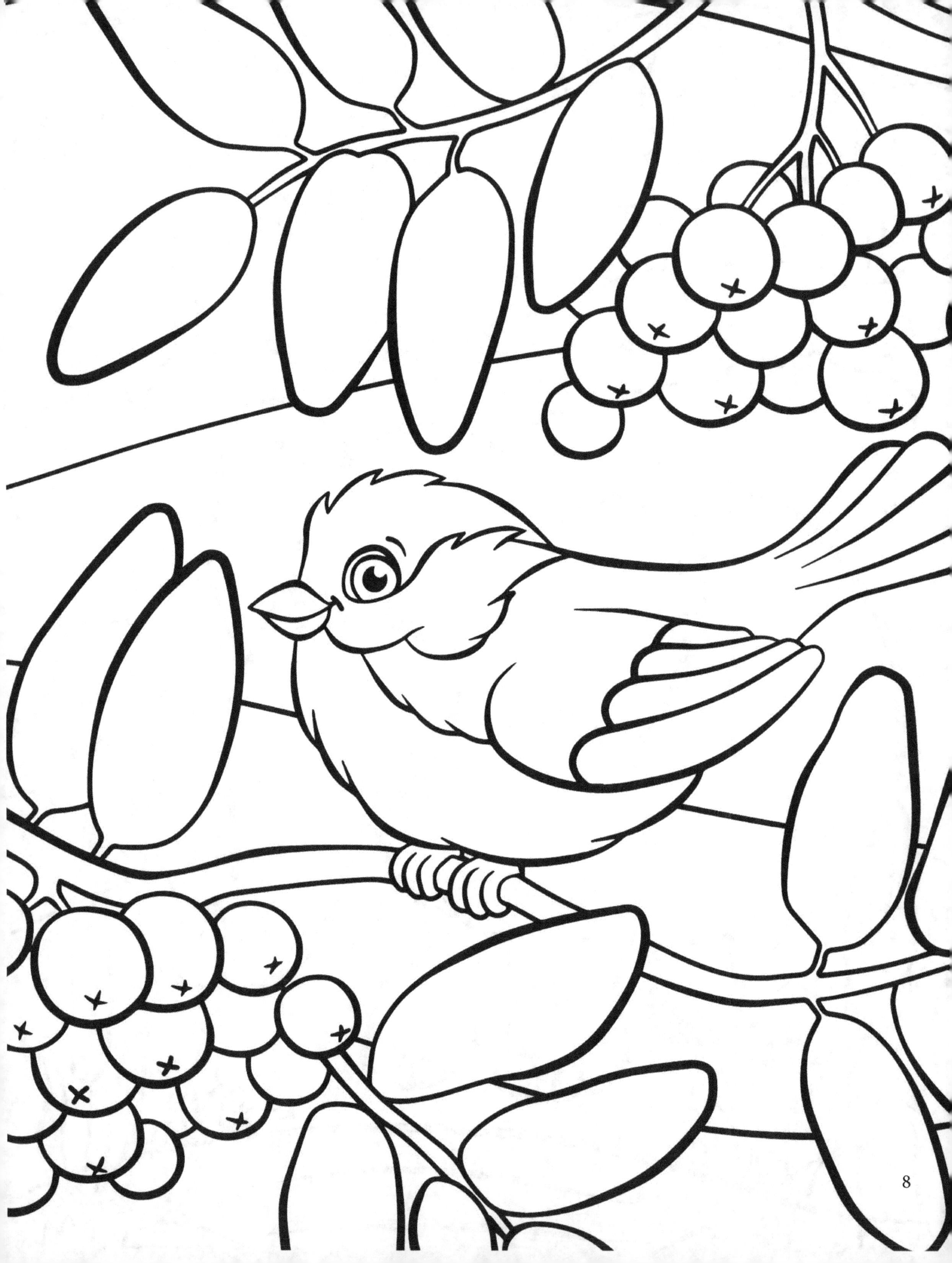

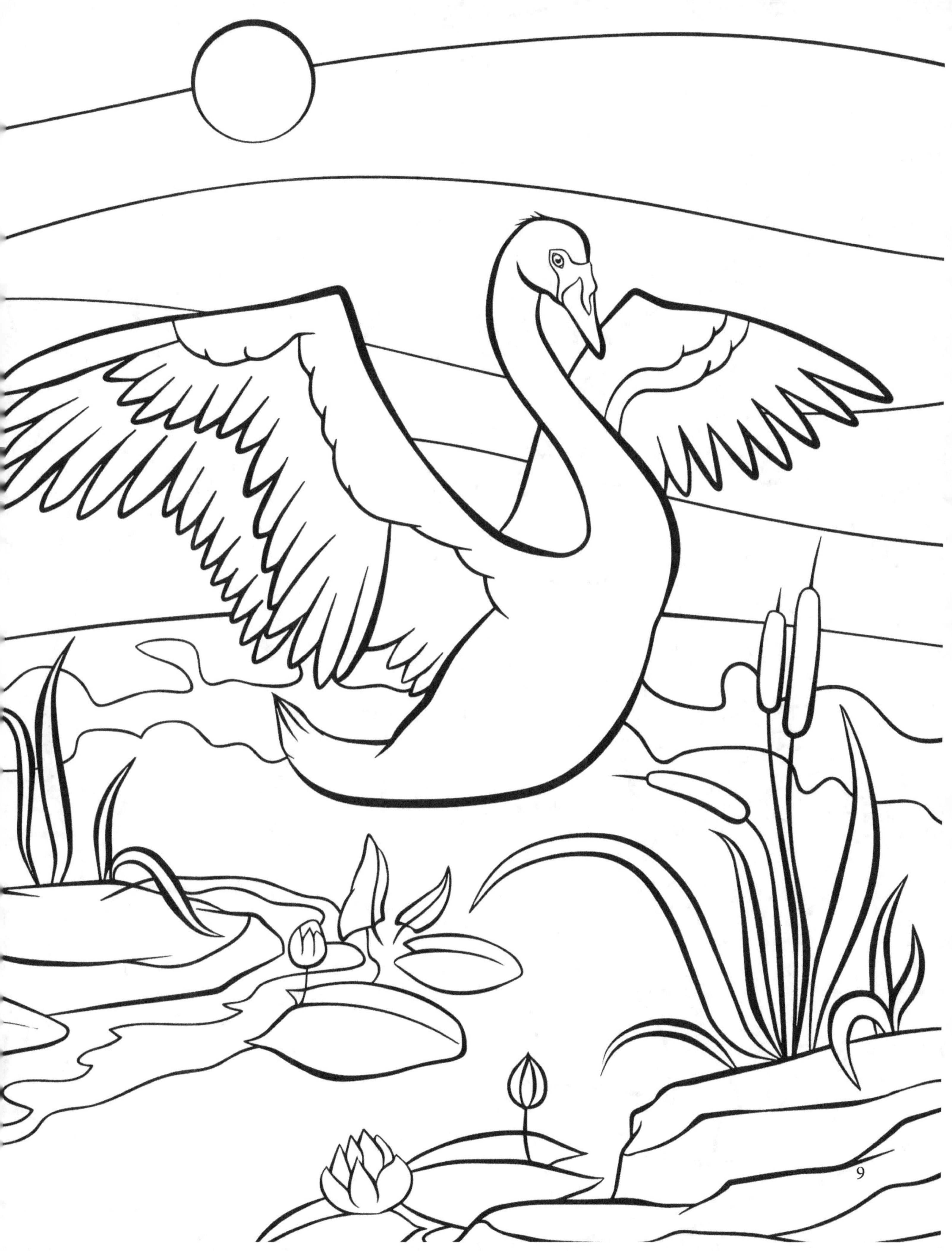

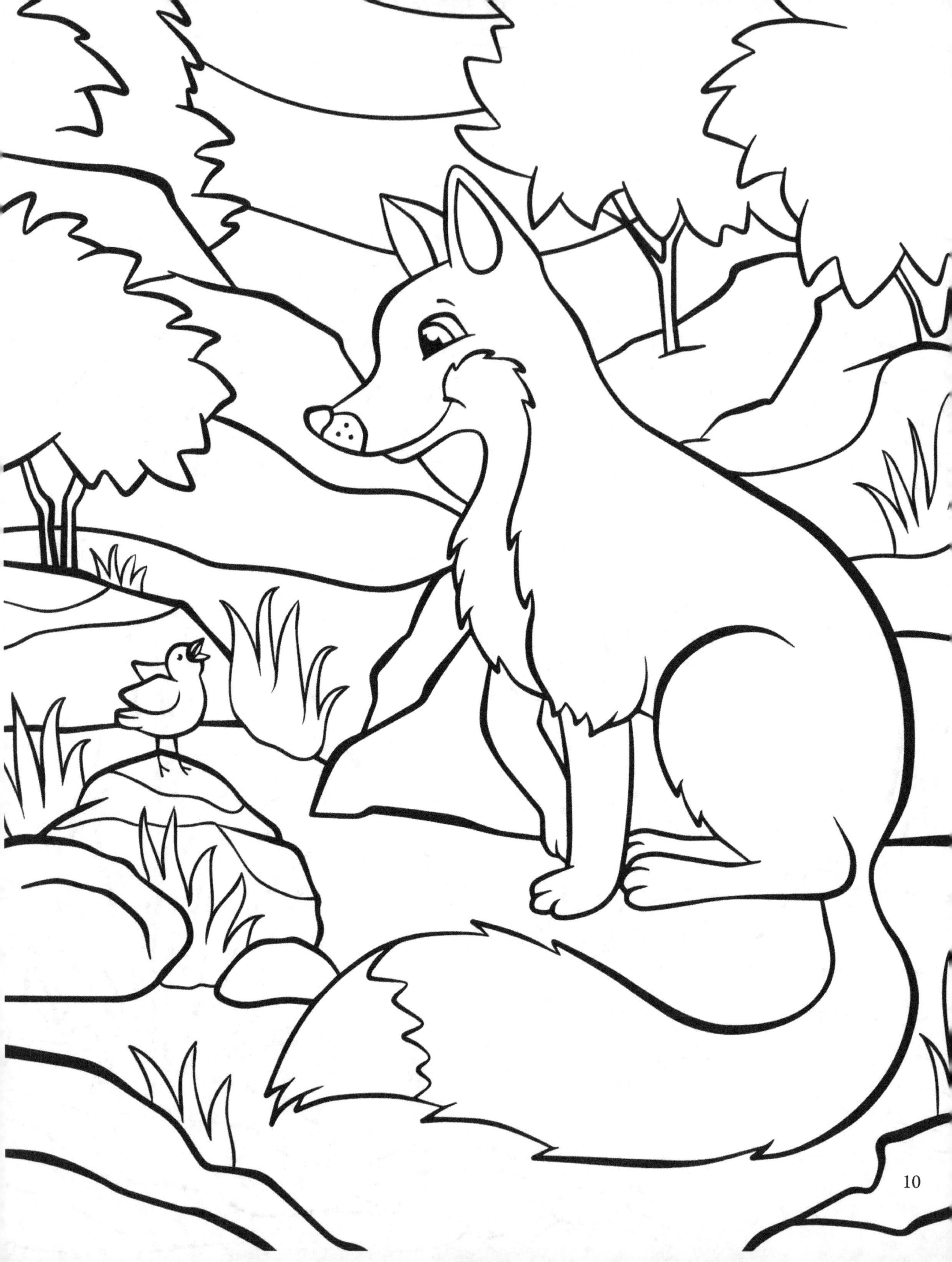

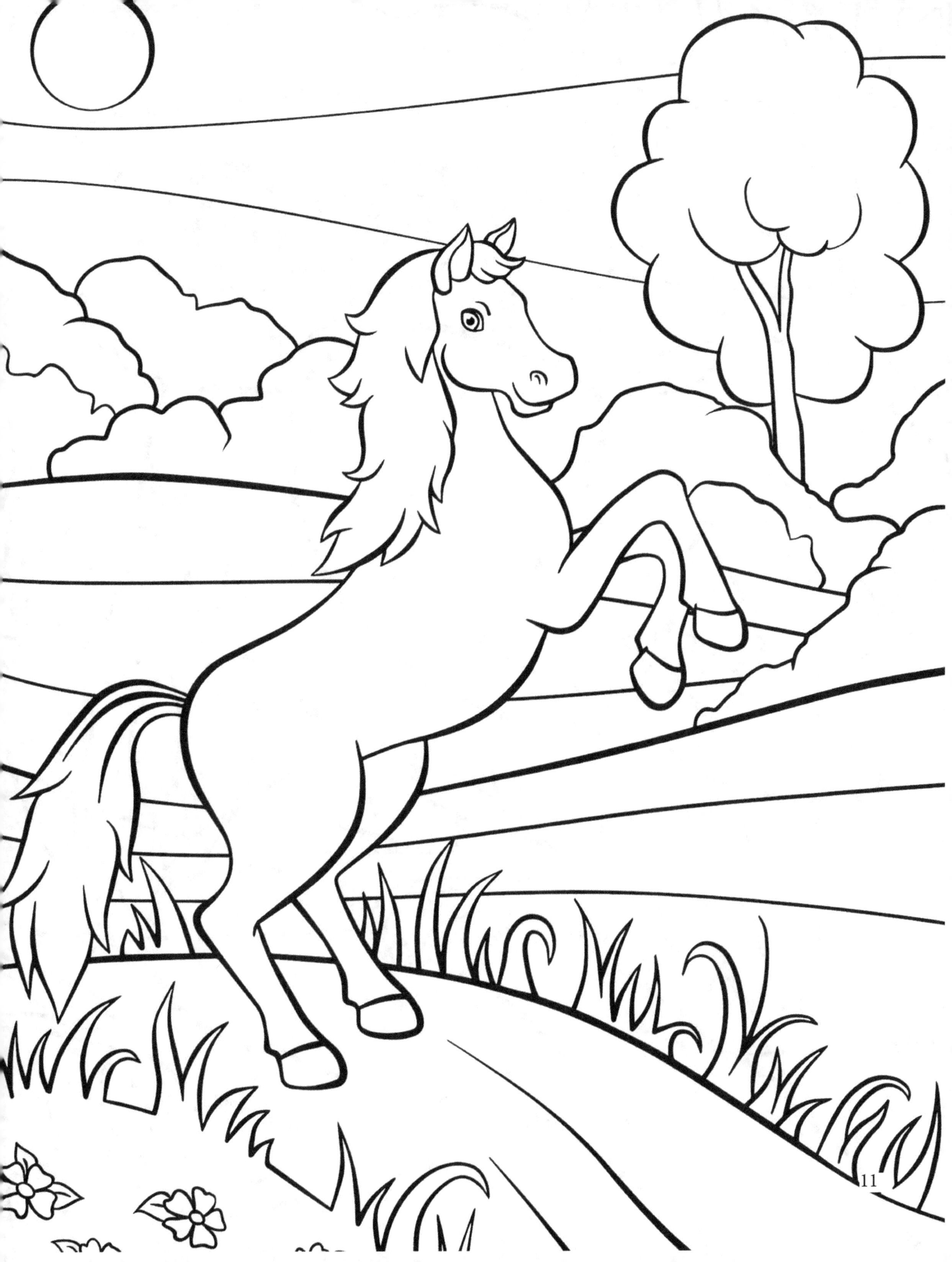

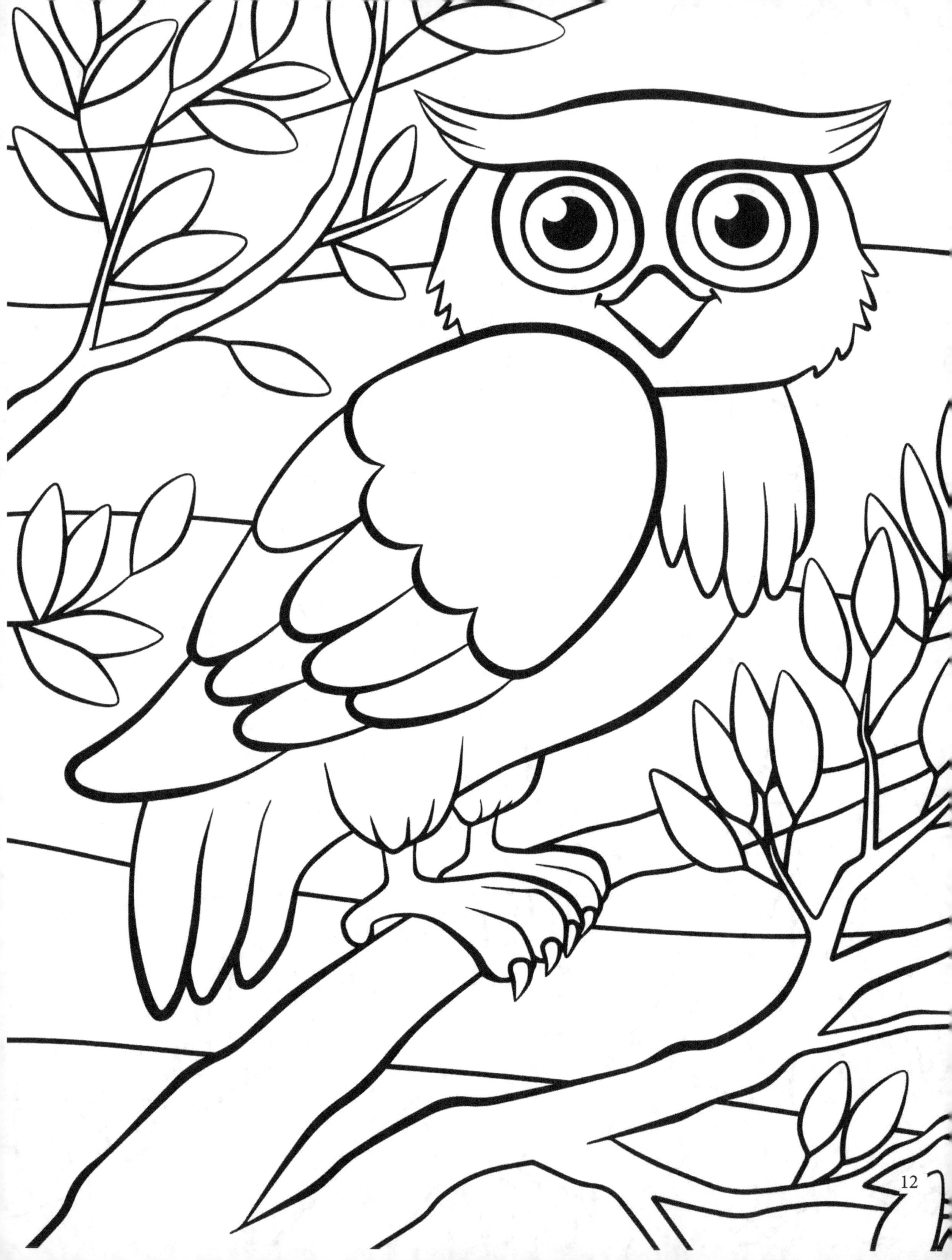

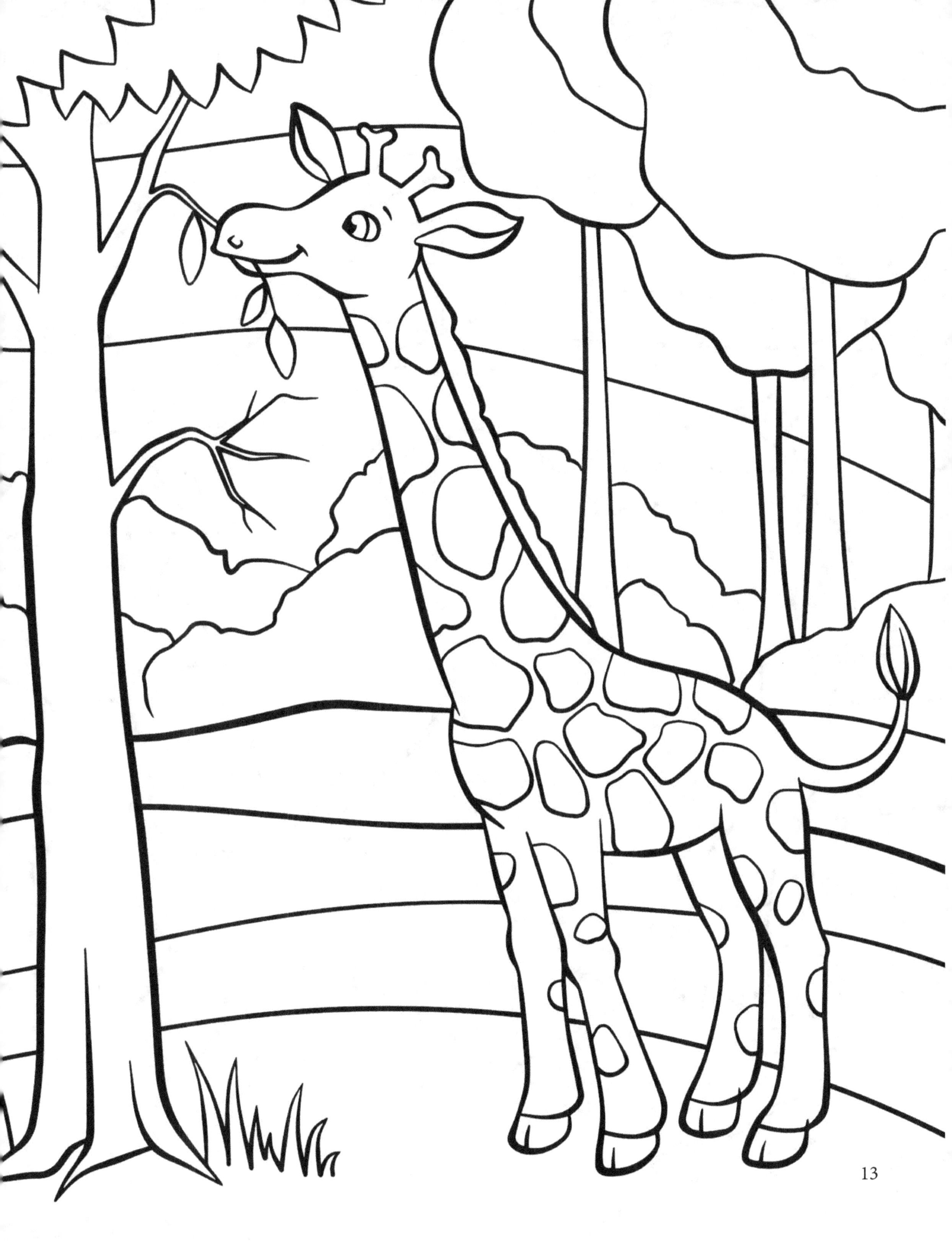

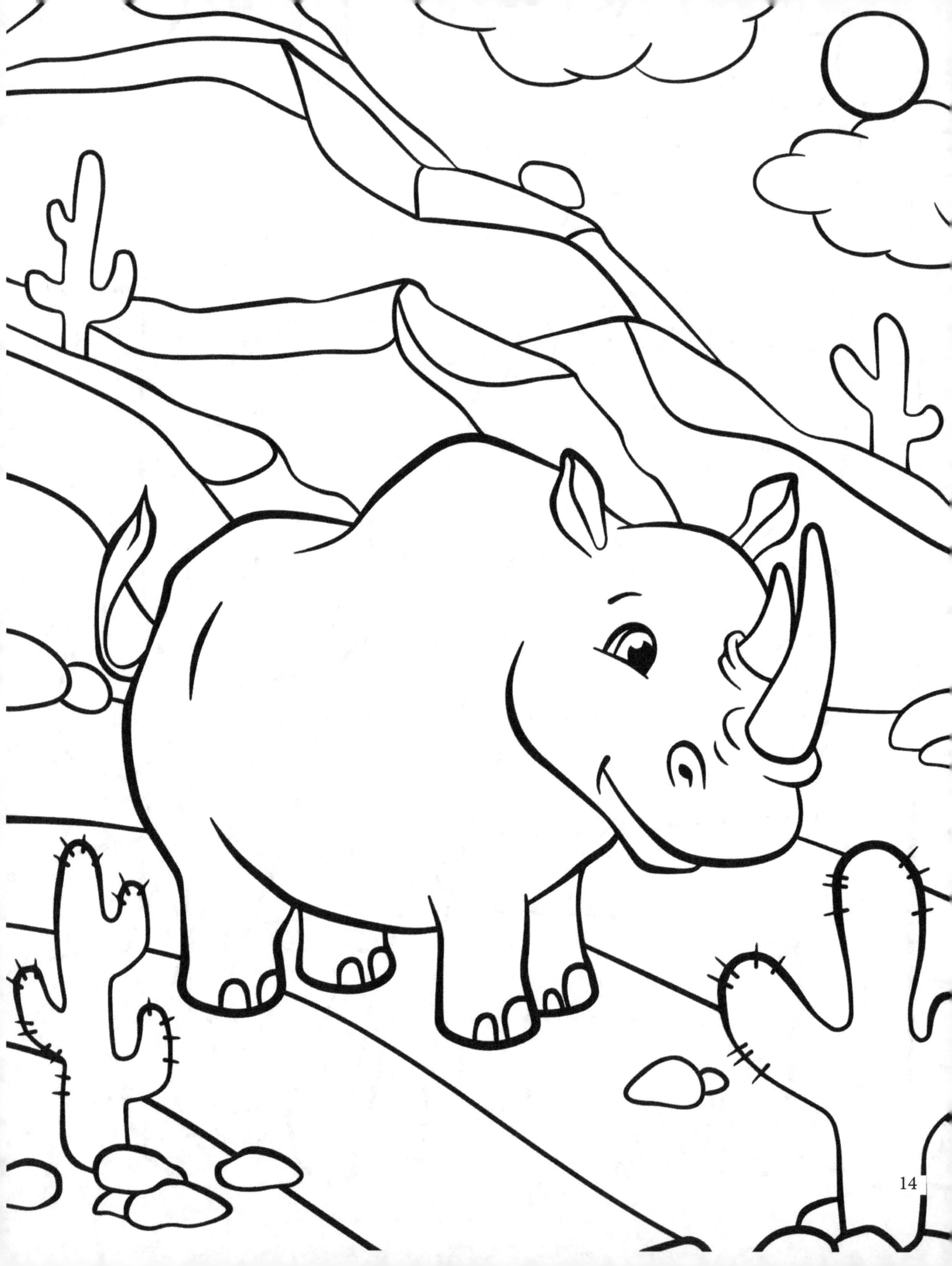

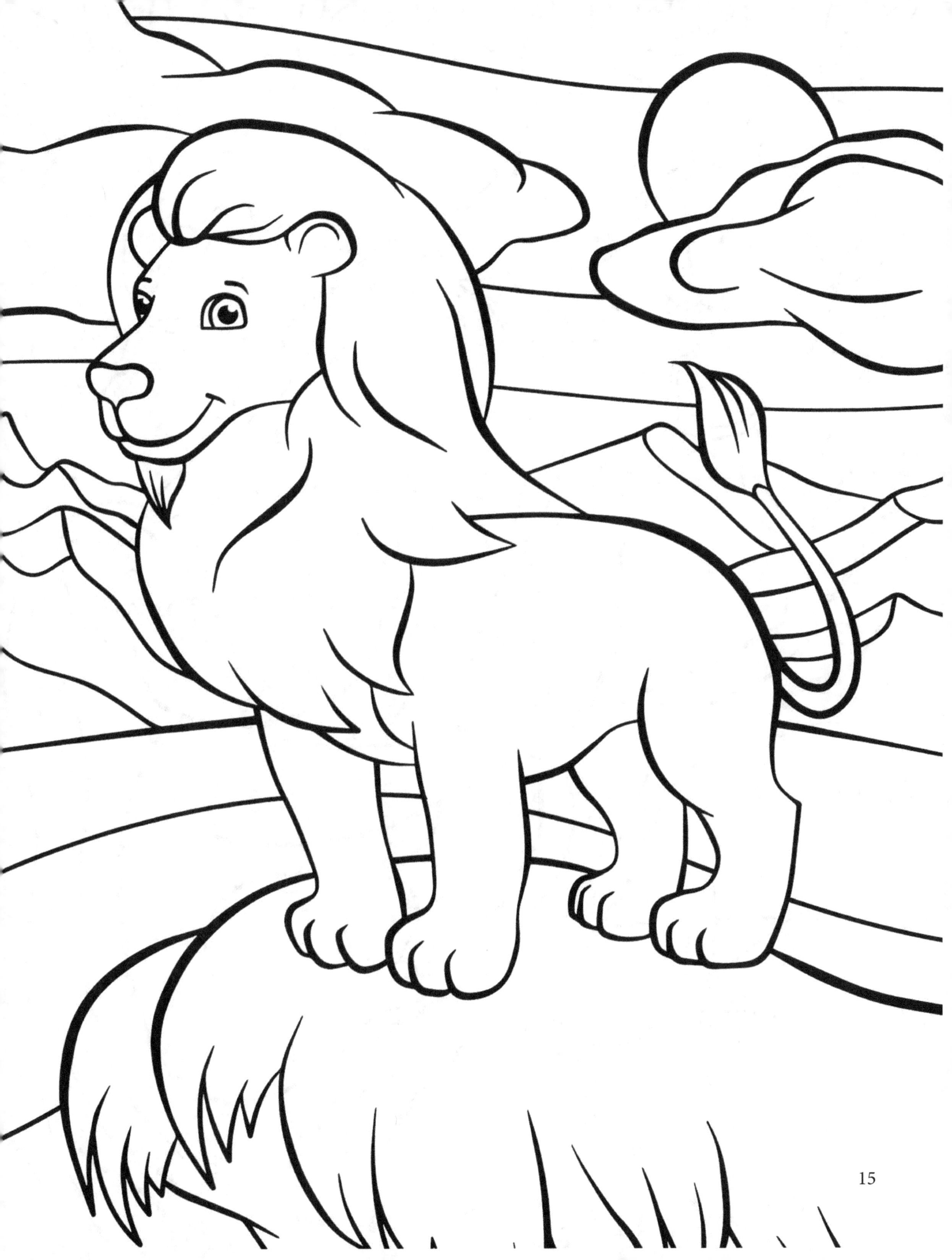

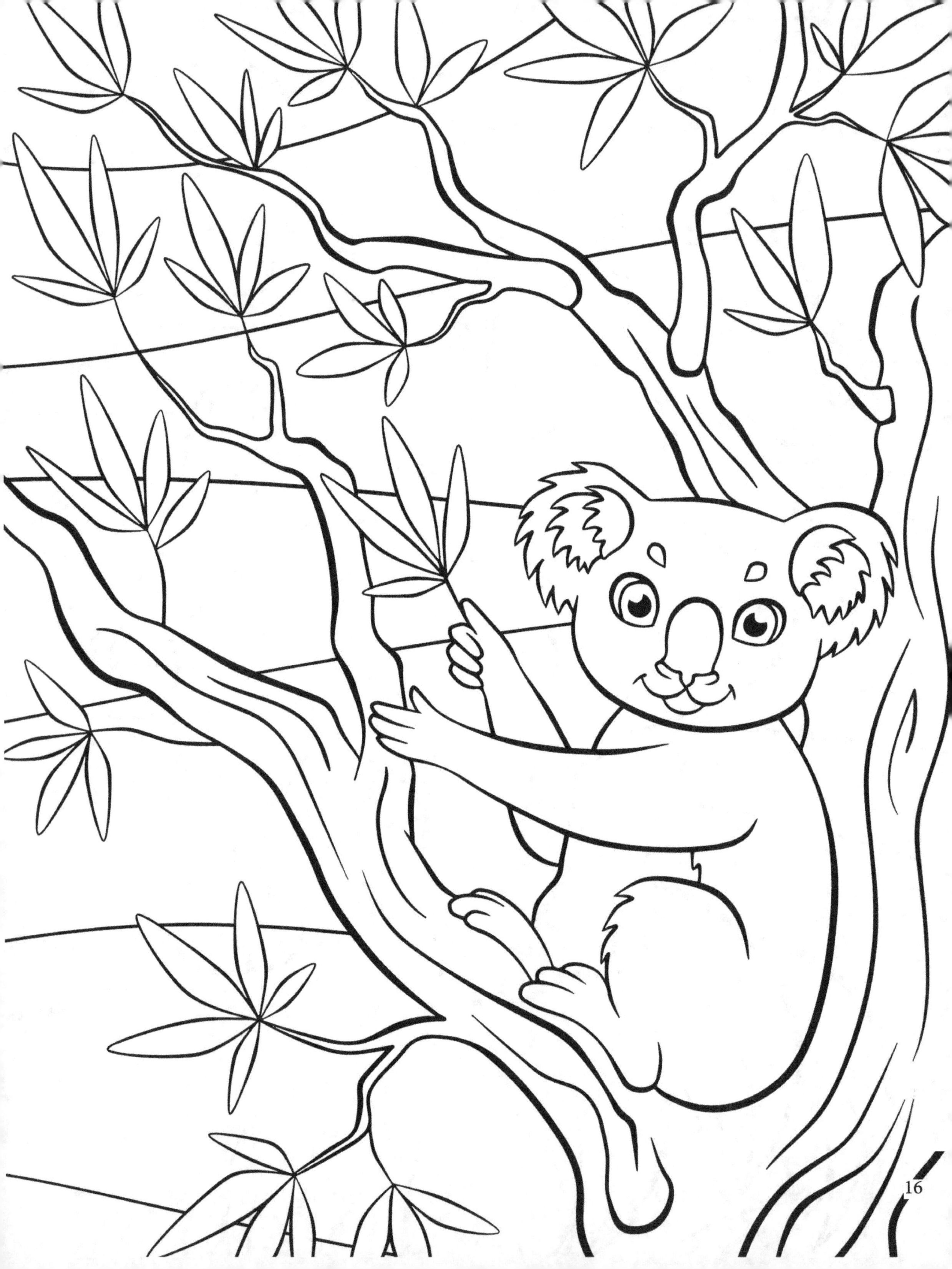

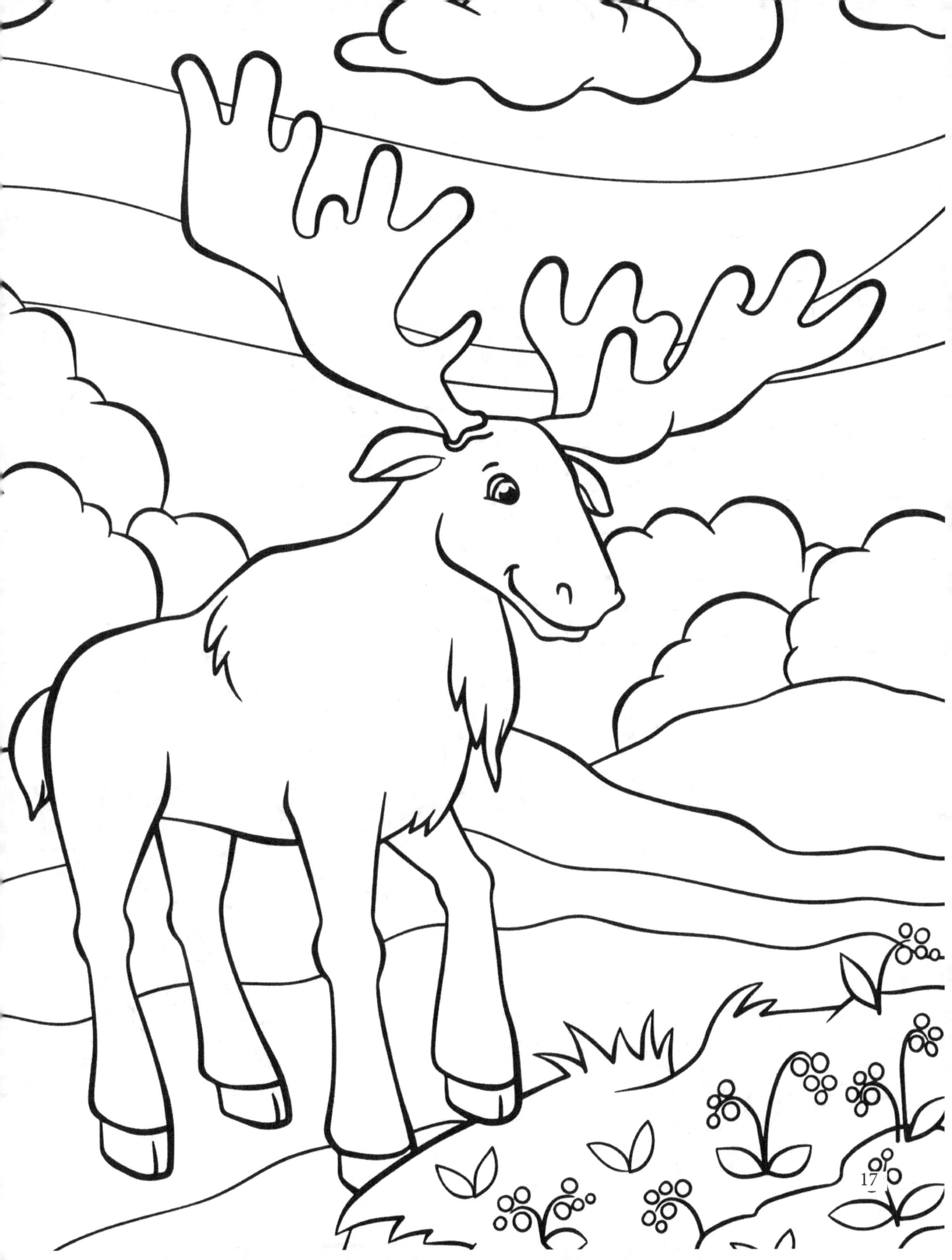

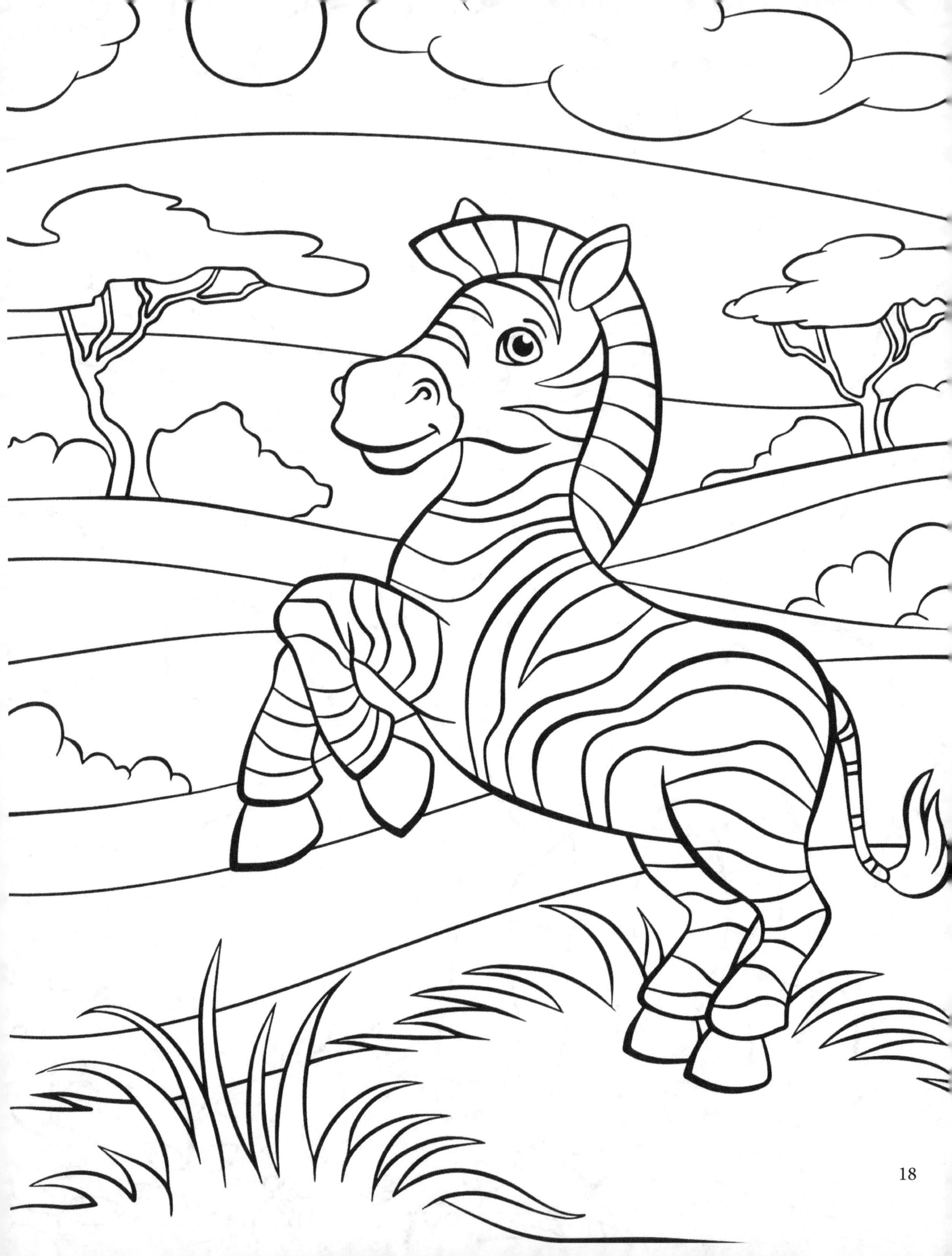

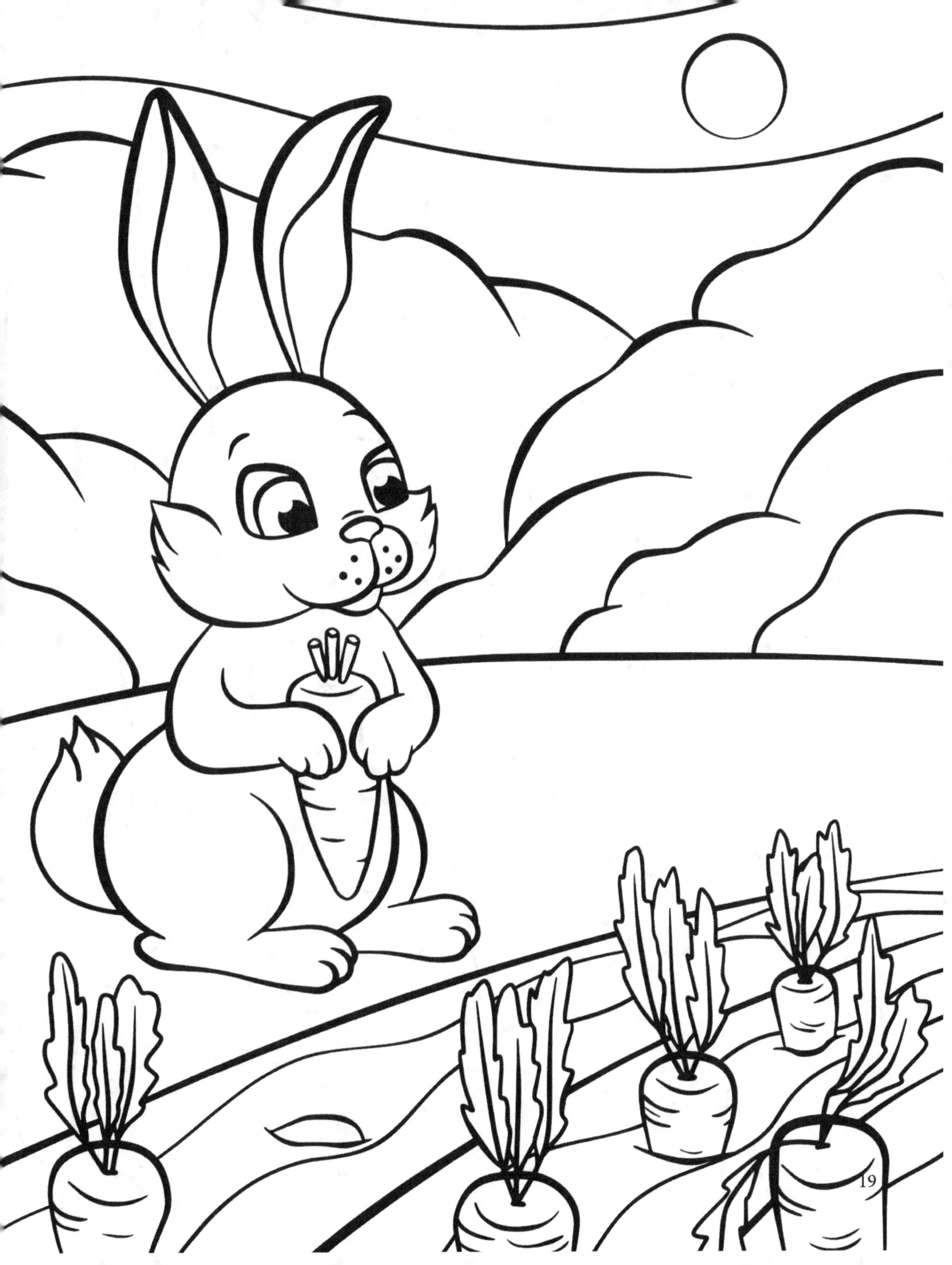

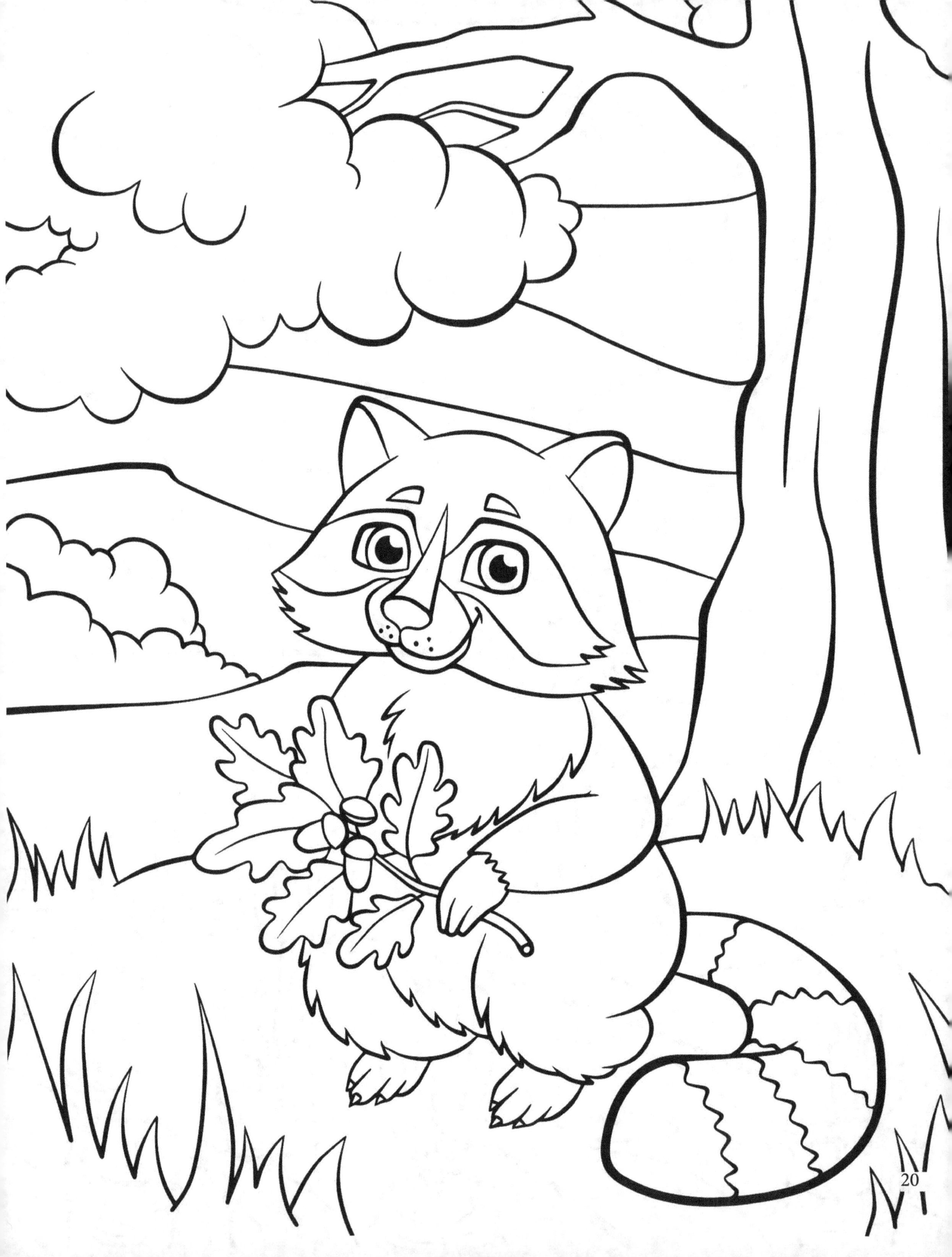

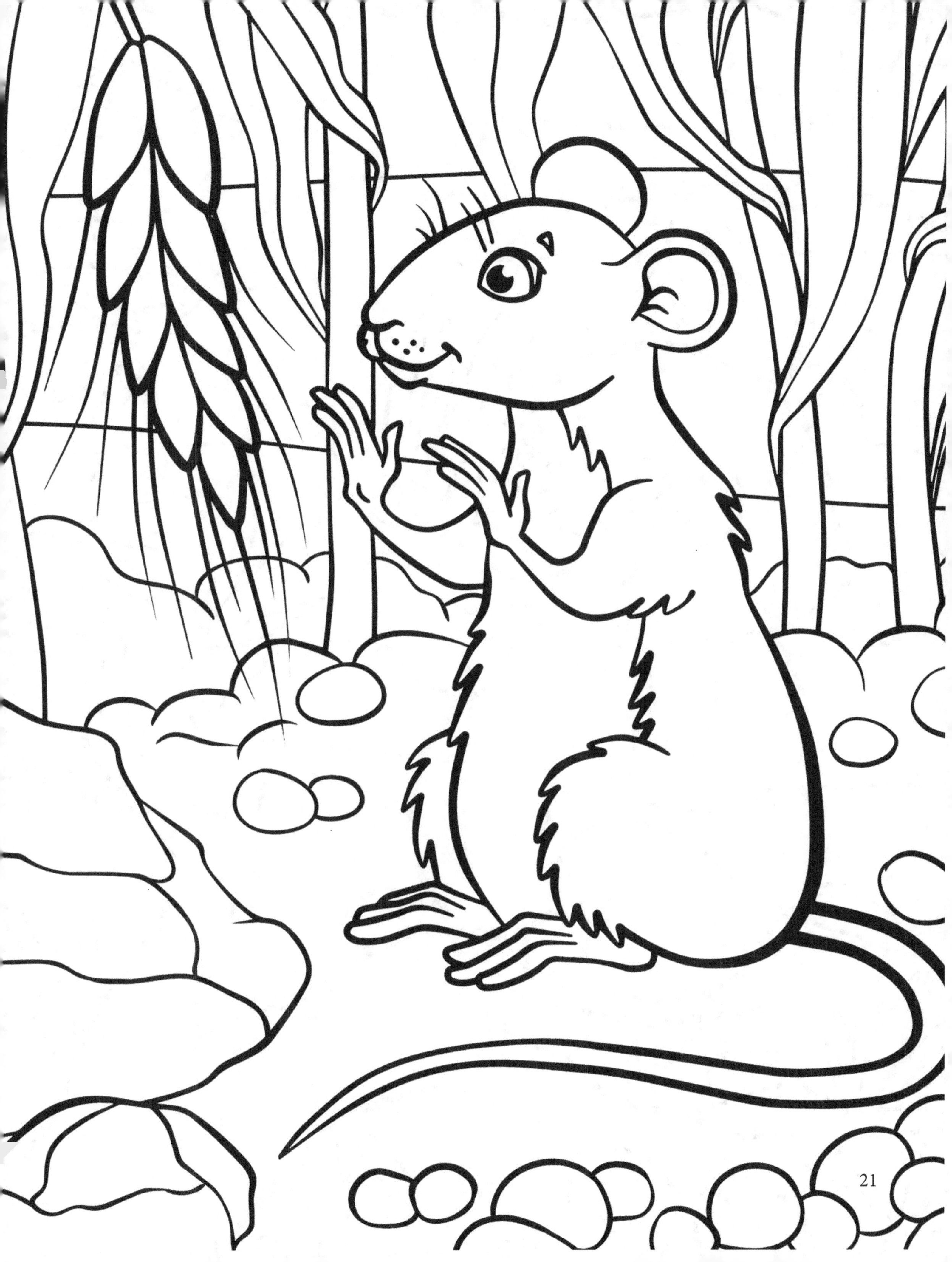

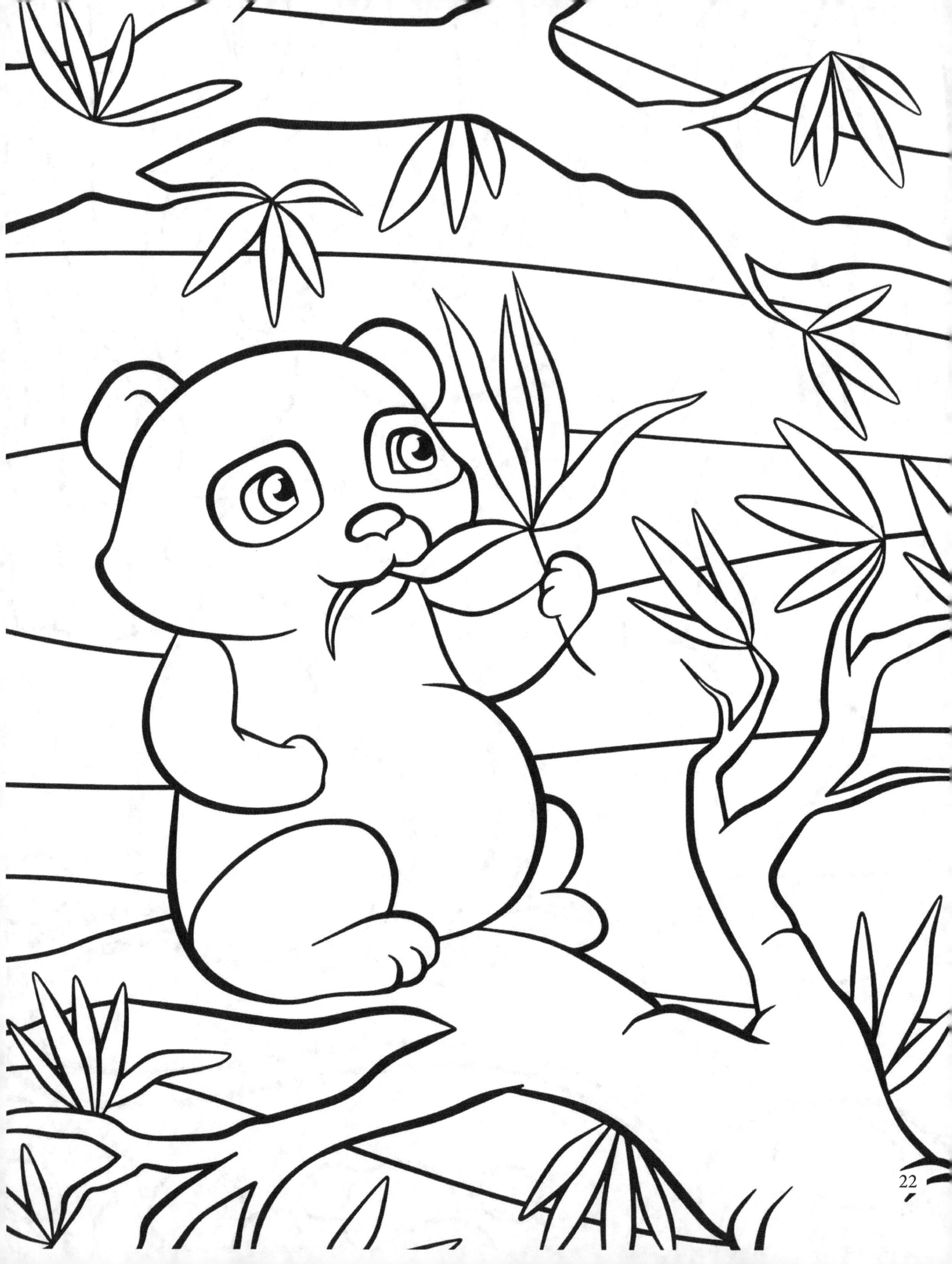

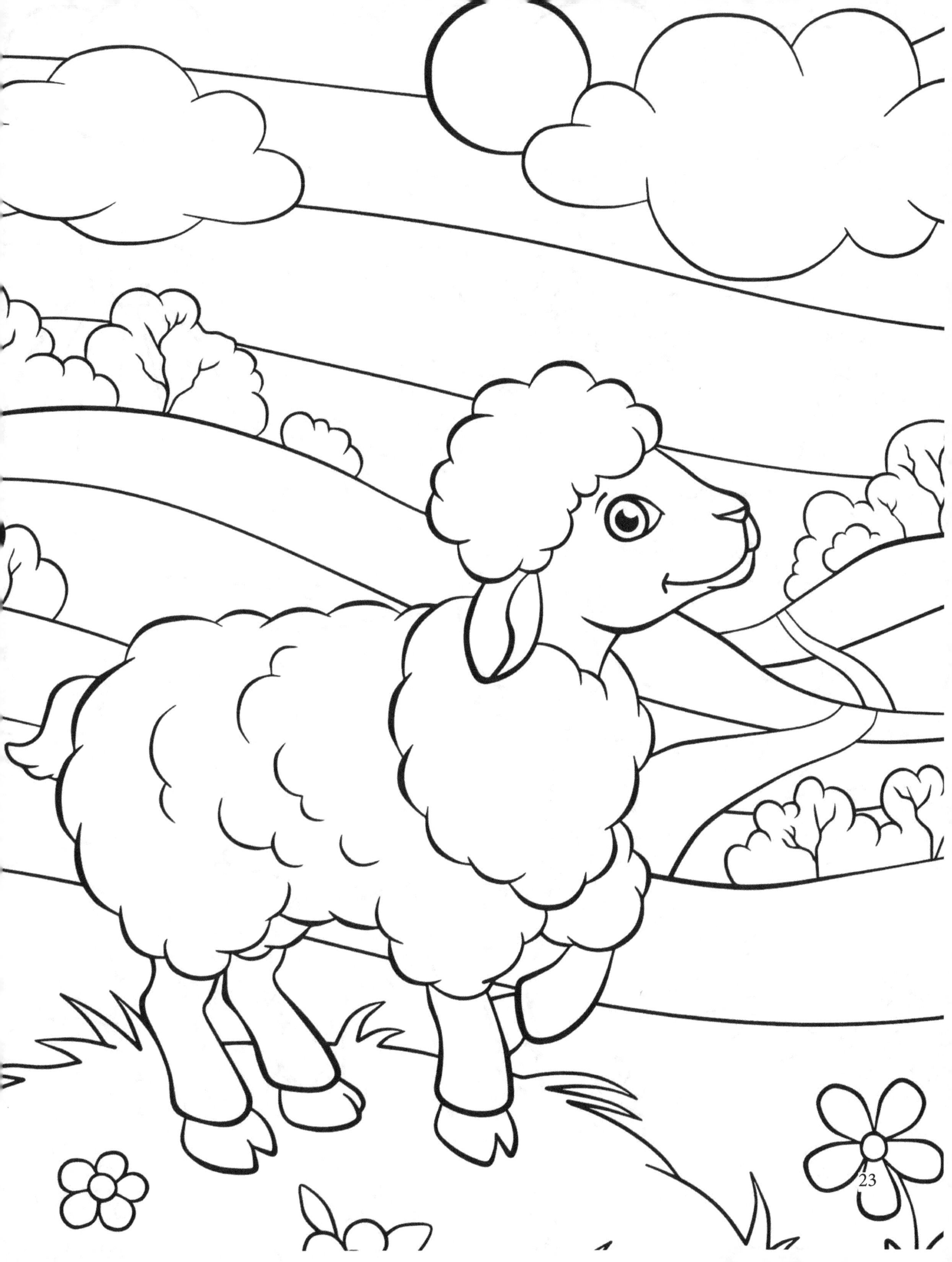

23

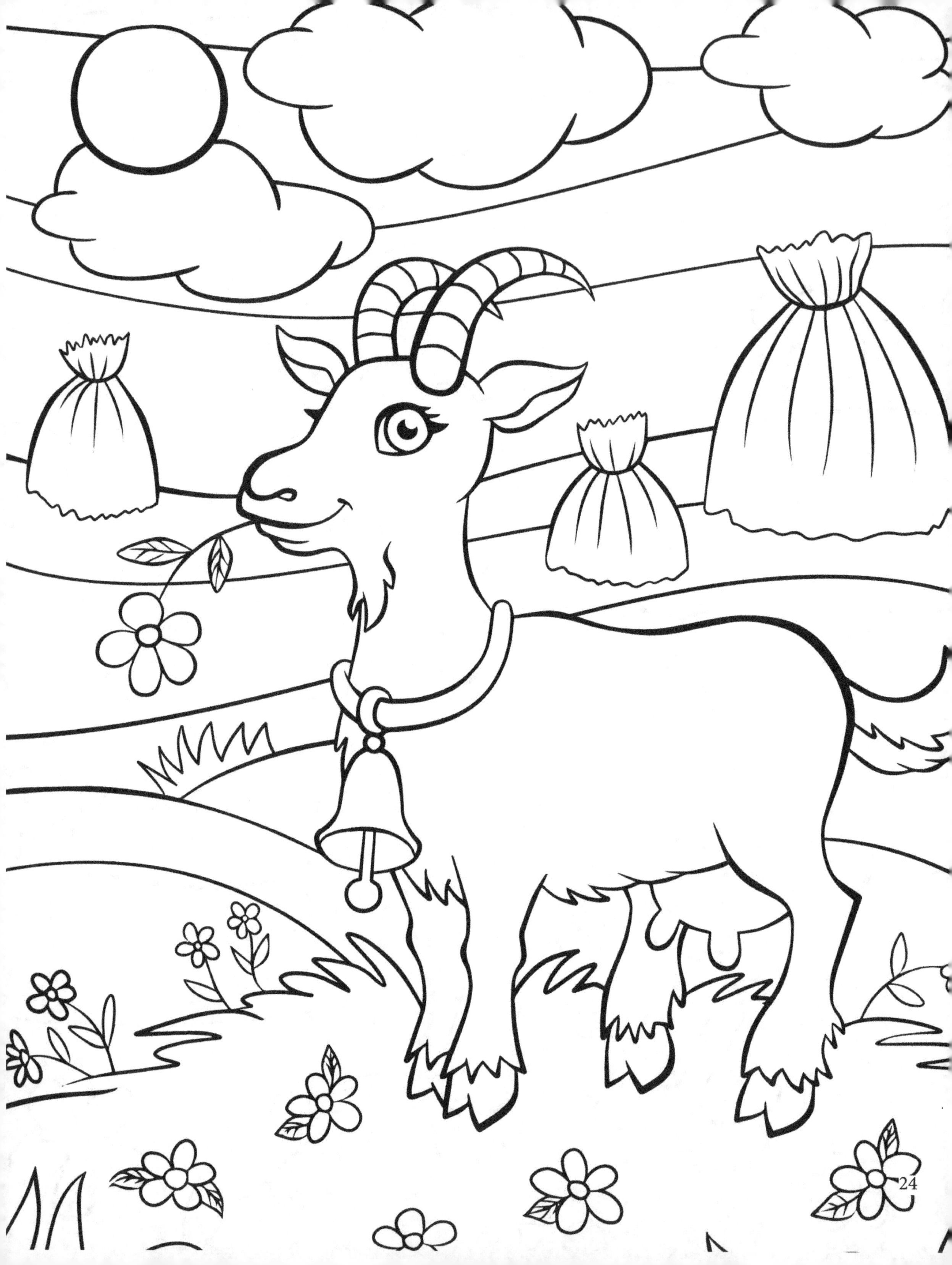

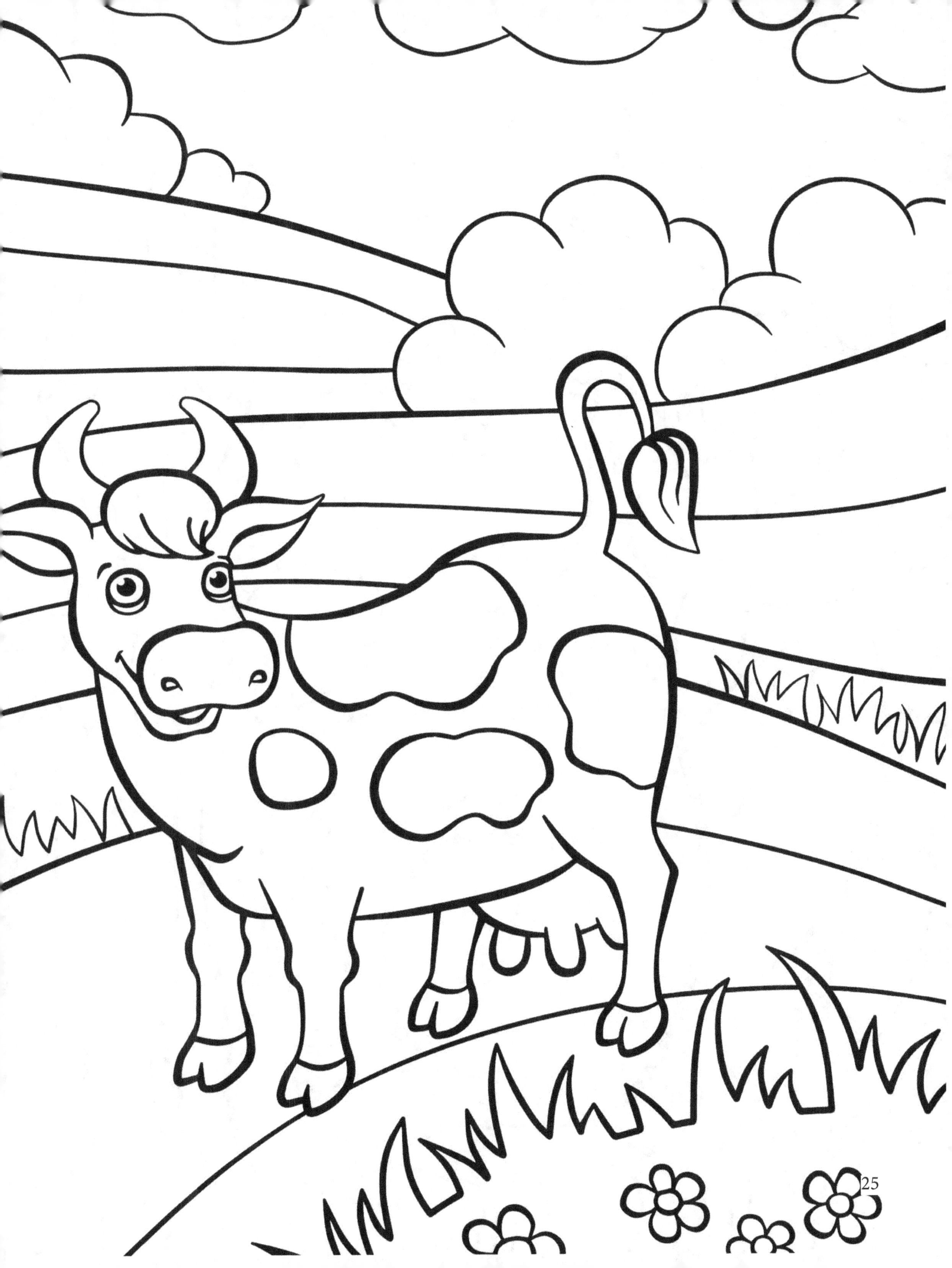

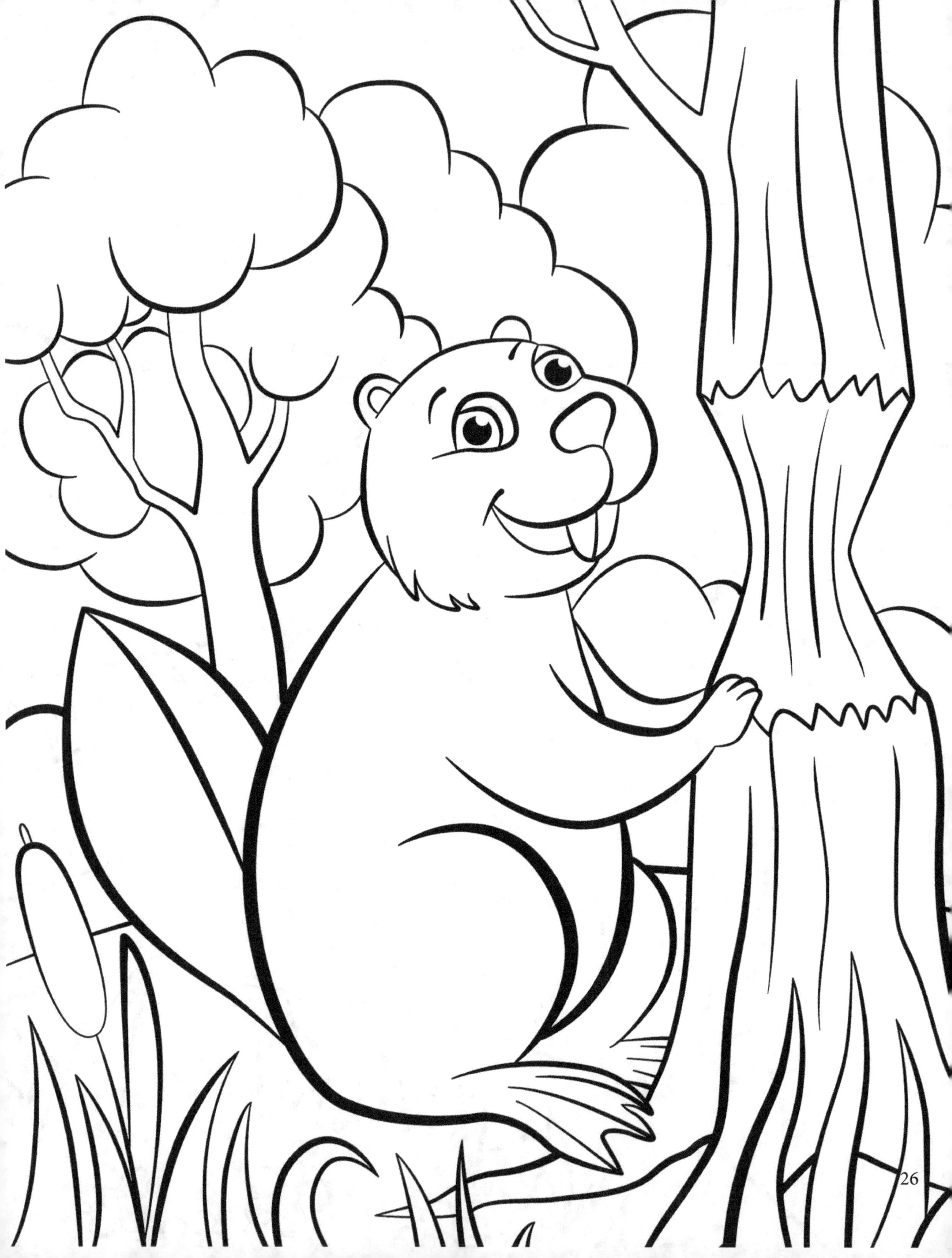

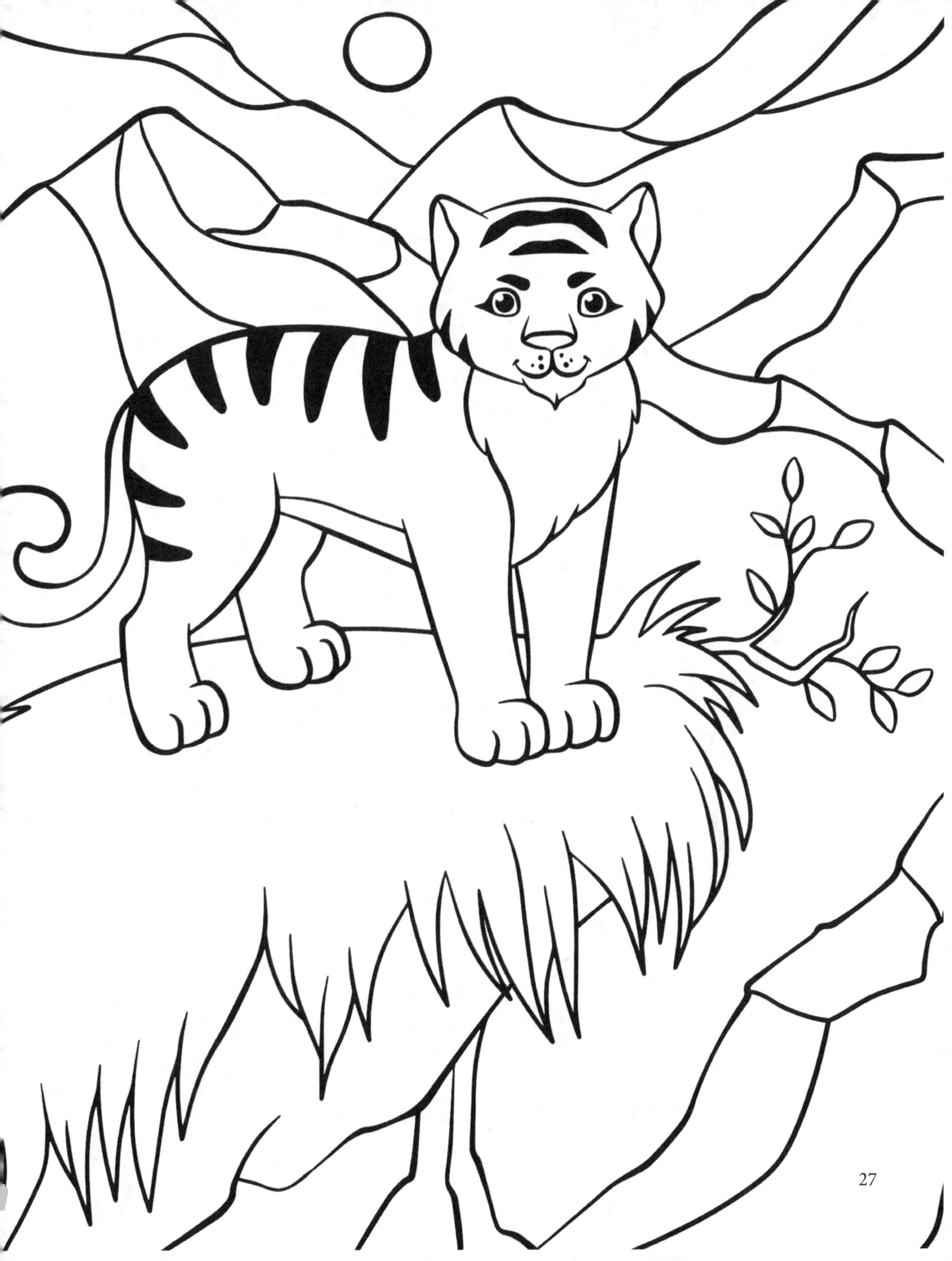

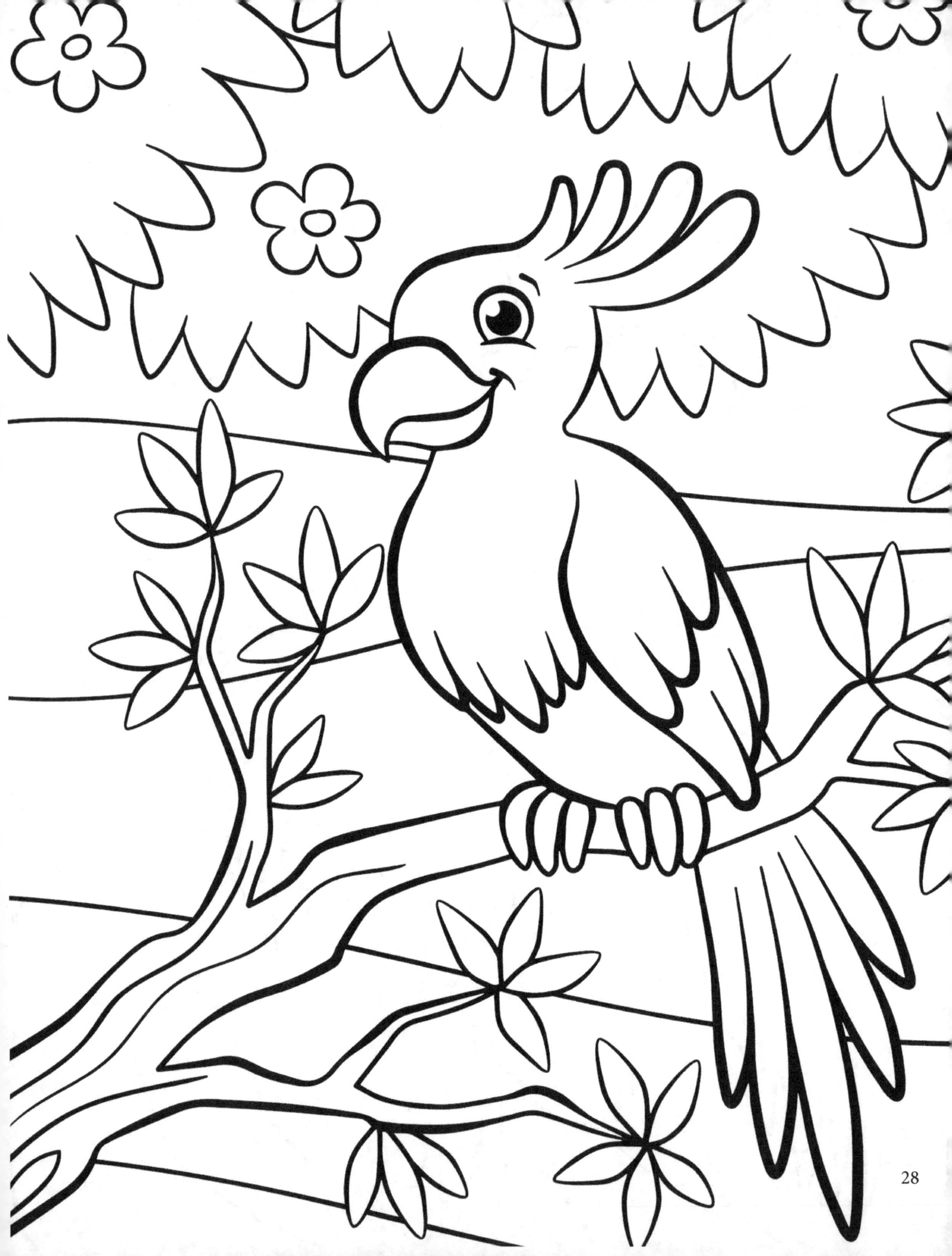

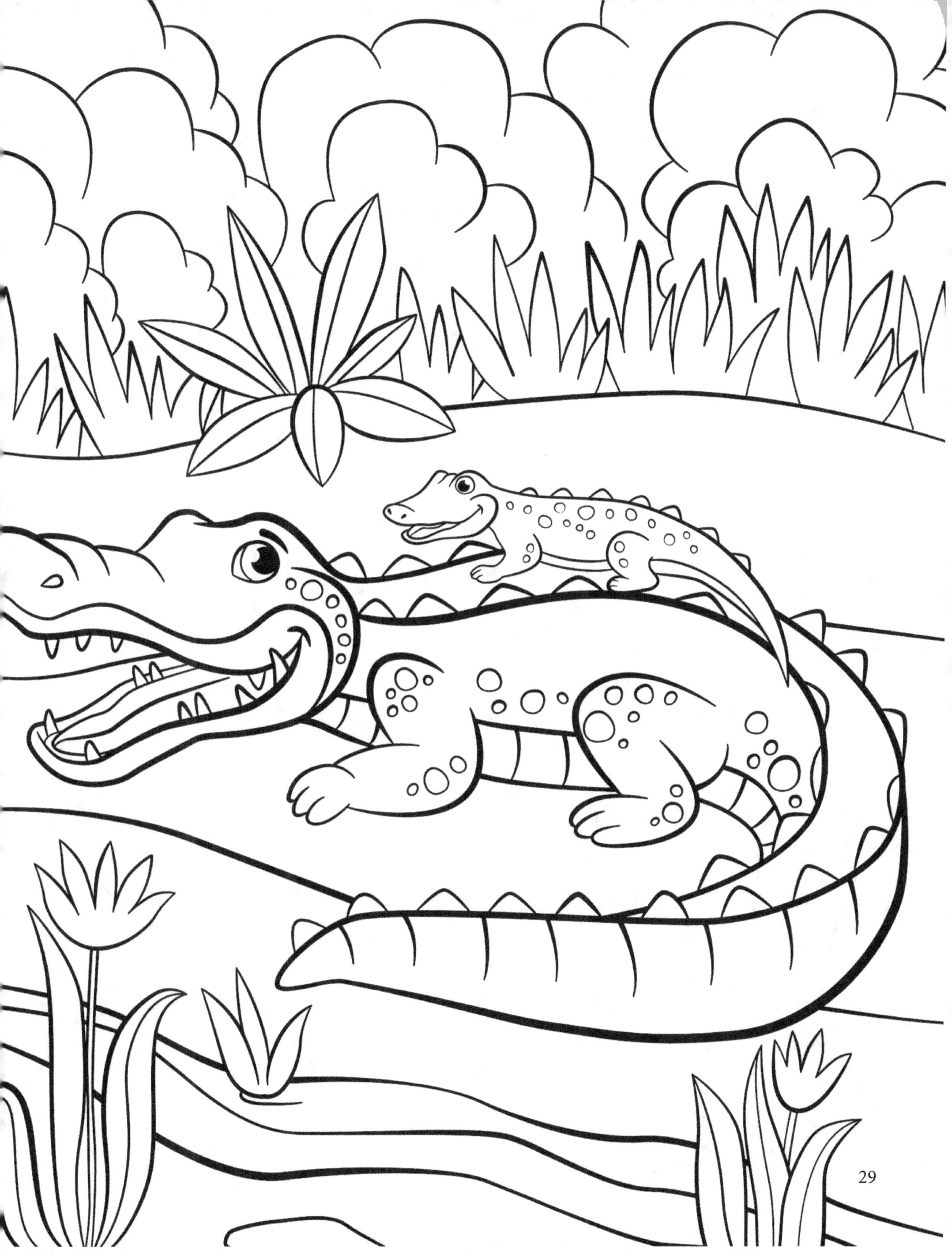

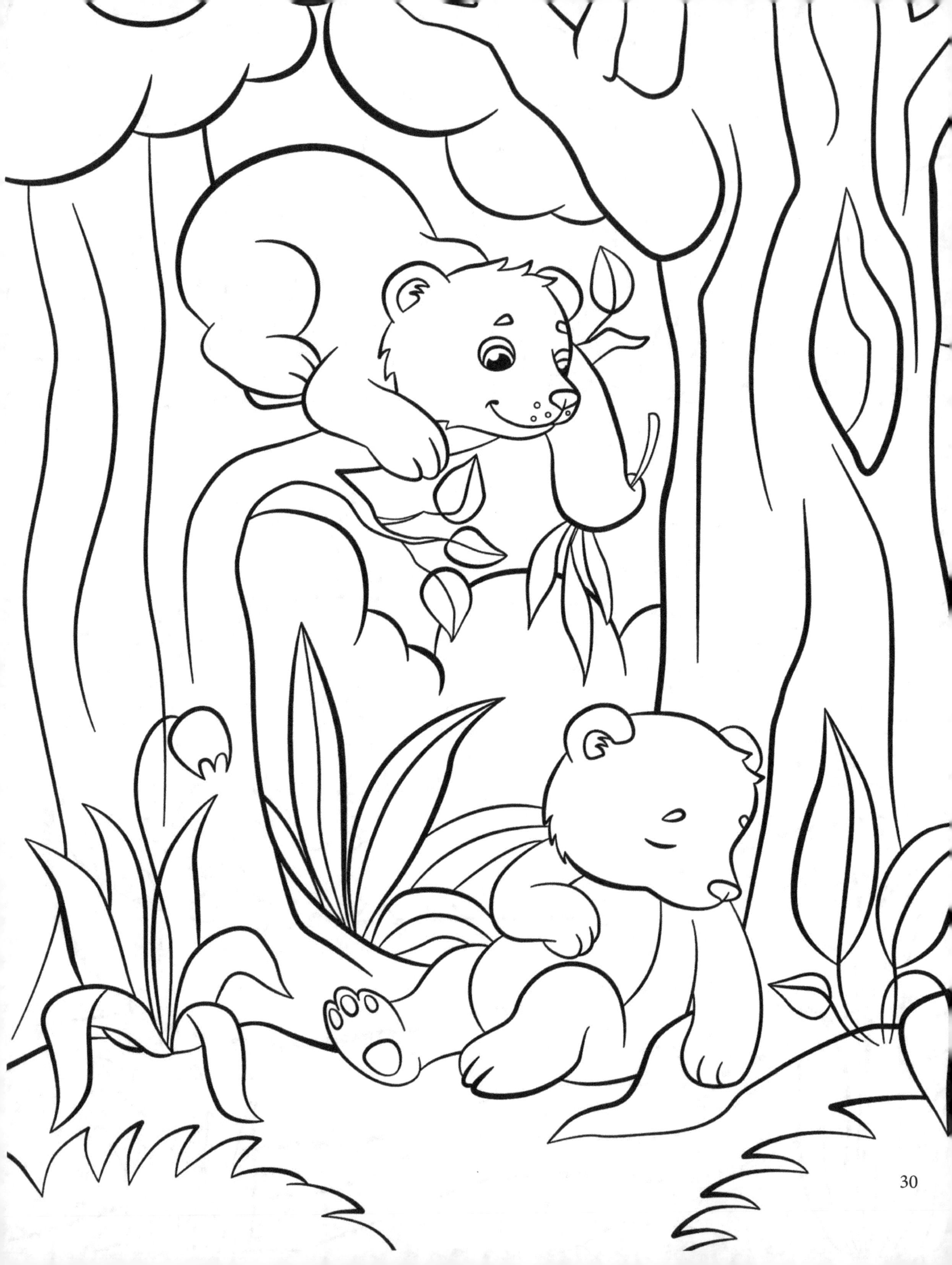

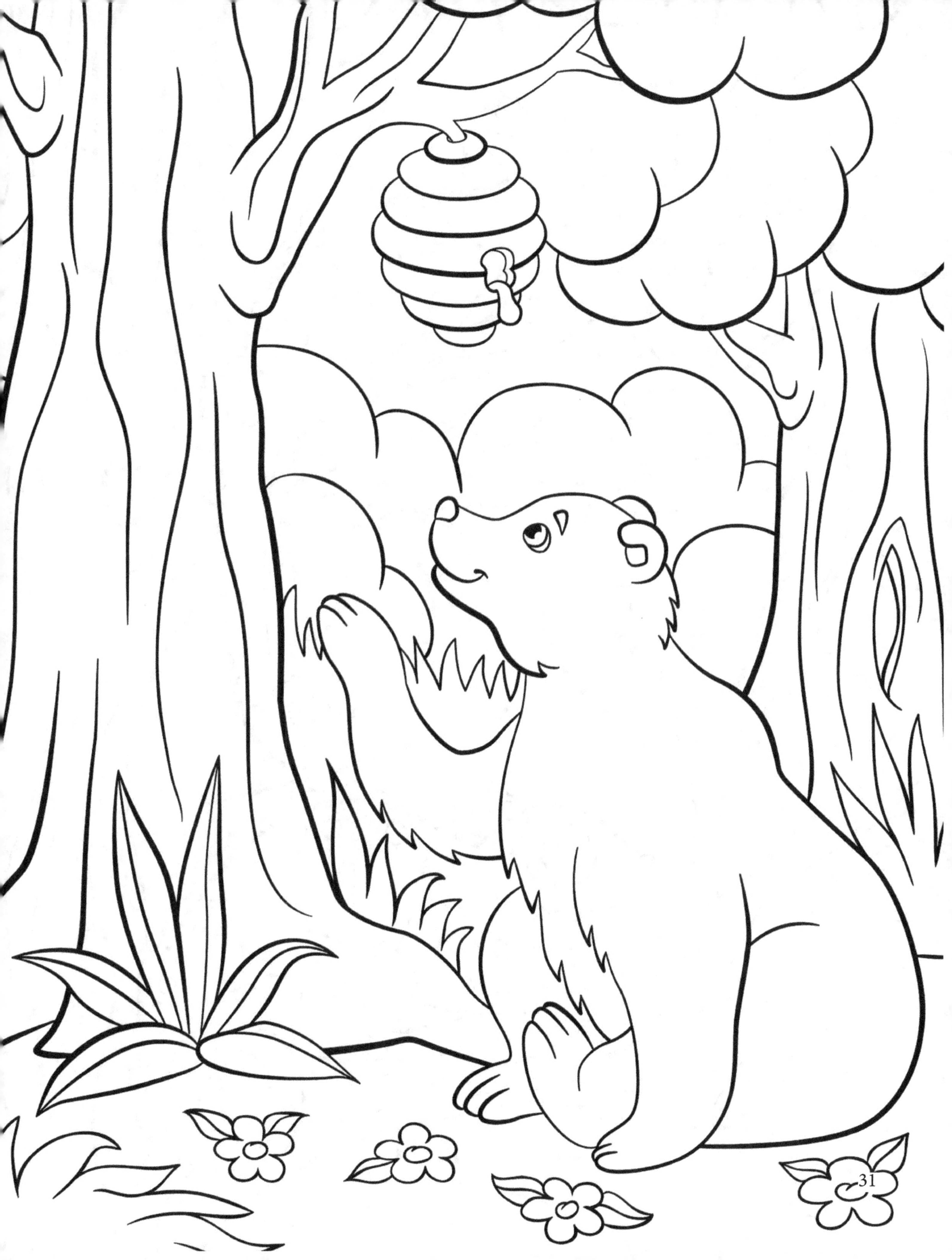

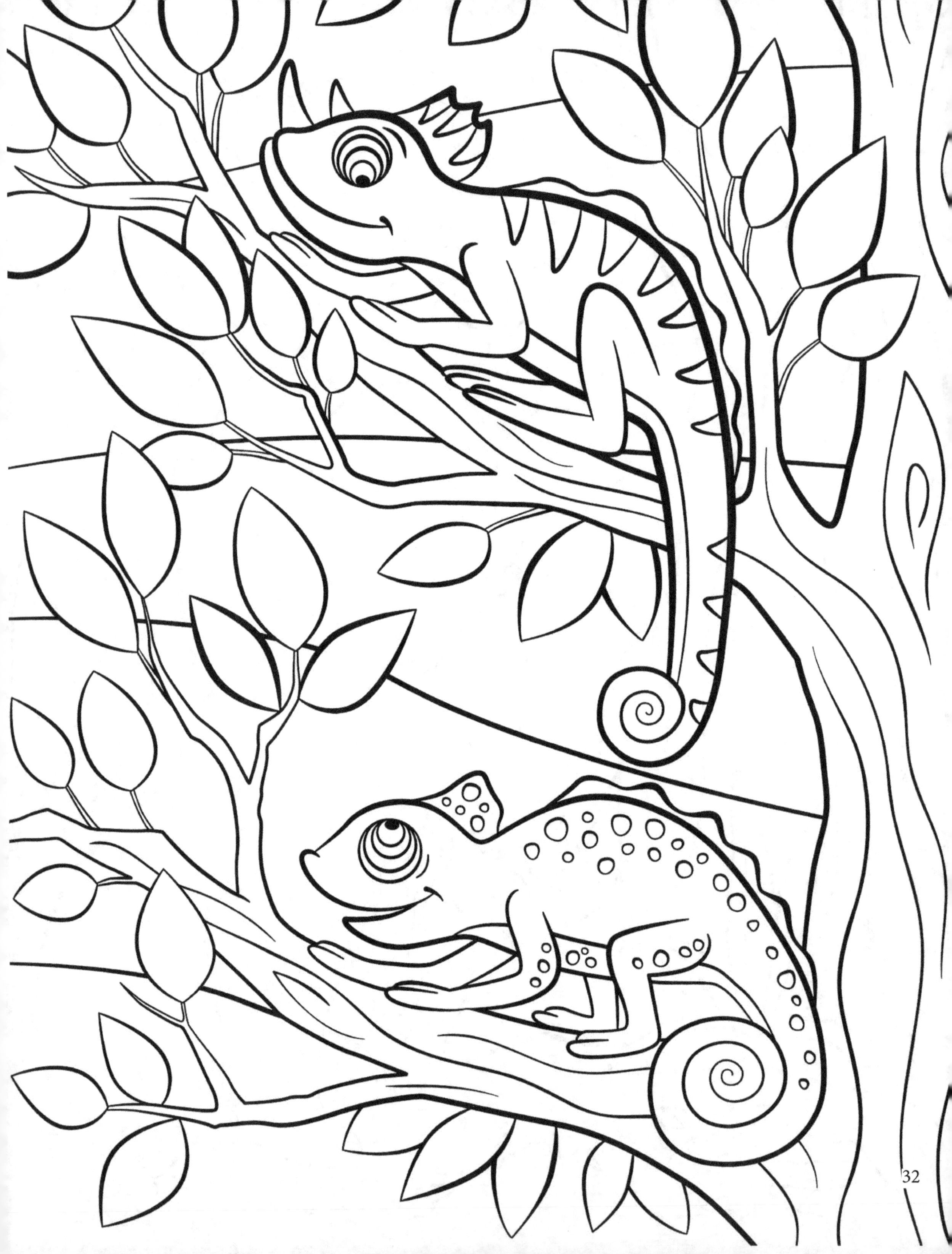

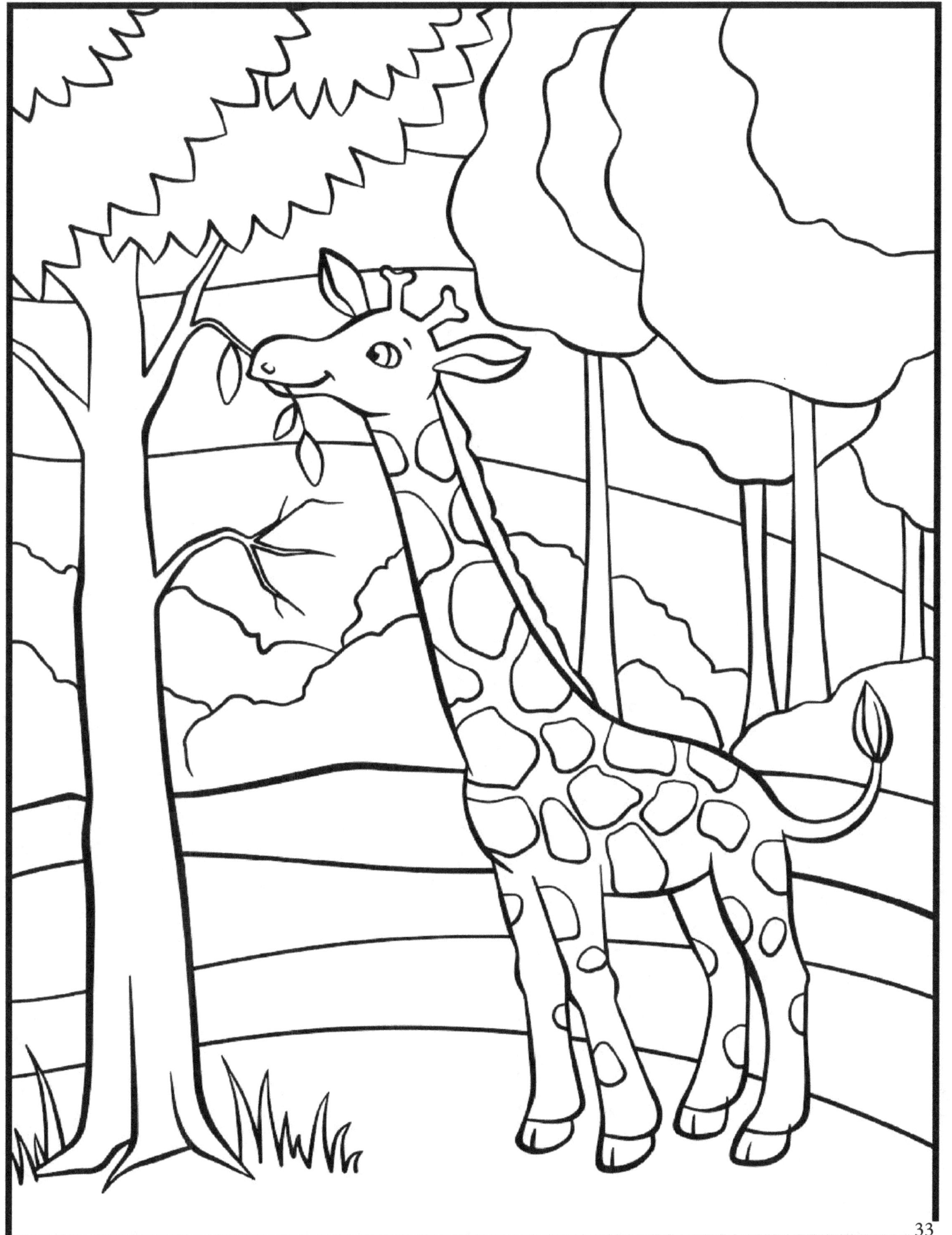